DEFYING GRAVITY™

Improve your vertical jump and more for volleyball

Nicolas Roy

Copyright © 2014 ::: All Rights Reserved

DEFYING GRAVITY:
IMPROVE YOUR VERTICAL JUMP AND MORE FOR VOLLEYBALL

COPYRIGHT © 2014 Nicolas Roy
ALL RIGHTS RESERVED

Cover design by Tristan Grégoire
Author photos by Annie Roberge
Editing and book design by Kelly Andersson

NO PART OF THIS BOOK MAY BE REPRODUCED OR TRANSMITTED IN ANY FORM OR ANY MANNER, ELECTRONIC OR MECHANICAL, INCLUDING PHOTOCOPYING, RECORDING OR BY ANY INFORMATION STORAGE AND RETRIEVAL SYSTEM, WITHOUT PERMISSION IN WRITING FROM THE AUTHOR.
fonctionsoptimum.com
888-627-4032
info@fonctionsoptimum.com

ISBN 978-0-9939792-0-0

Printed in the United States of America
13 14 15 16 17 18   10 9 8 7 6 5 4 3 2 1

CONTENTS

DEFYING GRAVITY	1
PLAYING DETECTIVE	9
YOU CAN'T FIRE A CANNON FROM A CANOE!	15
STABILIZE THE CANOE WITH 22 GREAT PILLARS!	29
ACCELERATION: A CAR WITH A BIG ENGINE AND A LIGHT FRAME	59
PUTTING EXPLOSIVE POWDER IN THE CANNON	81
BOUNCE BACK!	93
CHOOSING YOUR ENEMY	103
NUTRITION, HEALTH AND RECOVERY MYTHS	111
WHAT'S GOOD TO EAT?	115
WHAT'S WRONG WITH THE STANDARD AMERICAN DIET?	121
ORCHESTRATING THE SYMPHONY	145
THE PERIODISATION PROTOCOL	155
ACKNOWLEDGMENTS	163

FOREWORD

A few years ago, I met Nicolas Roy, a young student/athlete at the Université de Sherbrooke where I started my coaching career. He was a highly motivated young man with a strong passion for excellence, striving both in athletics and academics.

Many years later our paths crossed again; I was a national team coach and Nicolas was leading our strength and conditioning program. Nicolas has had a strong role in Team Canada Men's Volleyball's recent success. He keeps our players strong and powerful, and helps them stay injury free. Nicolas planned, researched, and created adapted programs that helped us perform with our complex schedule.

Volleyball poses many challenges when we are trying to perform at the highest level. Keeping our athletes at peak form and injury free is a continuous challenge.

Nicolas Roy works hard to improve our players' state of physical readiness, by emphasizing the periodization of training – but he also considers many other aspects of their physical performance. He's a pleasure to work with.

In this book, he demonstrates his vision of the strength and conditioning aspects of movement, nutrition, and regeneration. Factors that are paramount in health and peak performance are discussed and explained in ways that facilitate comprehension by both athletes and coaches. I believe this book will explain and help you appreciate our volleyball training environment!

Glenn Hoag
Head coach men's Volleyball Canada

DEFYING GRAVITY

As a volleyball player, who are you?
And how important is vertical jump in your game?

Volleyball is not just a game about jumping high, but improving vertical jump will help most players. There are some things in life that we can never have too much of, and for volleyball players, jumping height is in this category. However, all volleyball players must know, with the help of their coaches, which priorities to focus on to improve their game. Here's a great illustration that was originally created by colleagues Charles Cardinal and Martin Roy. This illustration, which was modified for volleyball purposes, will help you keep in mind the big picture of sport performance requirements.

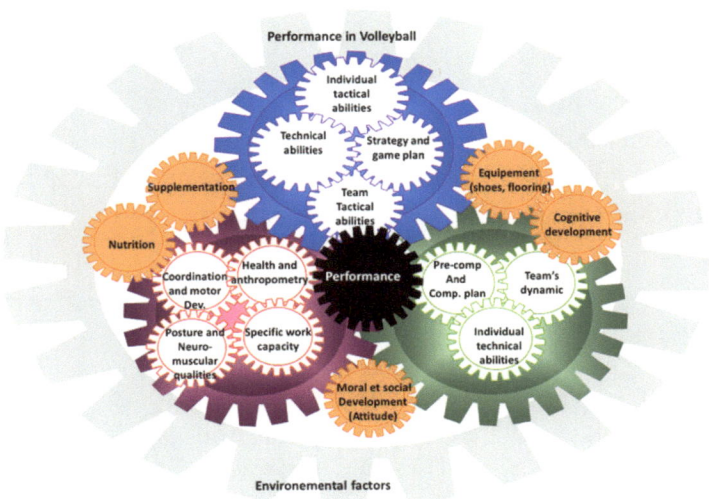

As shown in this picture, vertical jump is a very specific aspect of a big-picture system. The illustration includes aspects of the purple wheel plus the equipment, nutrition, and supplementation. Although vertical jumping is a goal in volleyball – because it's important for almost all positions and it's one of the most spectacular aspects of the sport – a player must not rely solely on that goal or ability. Many volleyball players follow "vertical jump programs" that too often focus almost exclusively on jumping abilities while neglecting other important aspects that must be considered for a volleyball career.

For example, I remember a player we evaluated in a junior selection camp for the national team. He touched 11 feet 11 inches, or 3 meters and 63 centimeters. He was by far the highest of the group. However, he didn't make the team and was sent back home because his volleyball skills weren't developed enough for the level of competition he was seeking. Though he will likely be invited for another development camp, the coaching staff just didn't have the time to coach him for that tournament.

Vertical jump is very important, but you can't focus on just that skill at the expense of other skills that are equally or more important. For many, it's about individual needs and a question of balance.

Improving vertical jump: part of the "big picture"

This focuses on improving vertical jump in "the big picture" rather than addressing just one aspect of it. If you ask a good coach how to improve vertical jump or strength and conditioning for volleyball, he will probably answer, "It depends." This is a very annoying answer for a motivated athlete: *It depends on what?* A wide array of factors can be considered, depending on the context.

Anthropometry and morphology

One of the biggest influences on athletic ability, relative strength, and center of mass positioning – and thus the vertical jump – is body composition. Most volleyball players have ectomorph morphologies (the thinnest of the three types), so coaches take for granted that their athletes have no body composition problem with fat accumulation because they are tall and skinny. While this might be true, it can also be false. Tall and skinny persons can also be considered as "skinny fat" if they have visceral but not subcutaneous fat accumulation. Because of their morphology, such athletes sometimes don't have enough musculature and strength to jump as high as they could. Some have postural issues caused by long levers. Because of their reach and their height, they surely jump and reach high, but on a jump mat, relatively speaking, they often don't do as well as smaller athletes.

For tall volleyball players, becoming stronger is not always their favourite activity;

> ANTHROPOMETRY: the scientific study of the measurements and proportions of the human body.
> MORPHOLOGY: a branch of biology dealing with the study of the form and structure of organisms and their specific structural features.

athletes usually like to do what they are already good at. Having long leverage from long limbs is not really an advantage for strength development or for flexibility –

but it is an advantage to generate speed at the end of the lever, as in hitting the ball. If those athletes persist in developing strength and flexibility, they then develop more power to jump higher, they diminish their risk of overuse injury, and they improve their work capacity to maintain their explosiveness for a longer period. Even if a volleyball player doesn't have problems with fat accumulation, he should monitor his nutrition. This is a serious topic for many reasons besides the obvious focus on body composition. Many volleyball players don't eat very well, whether it's lack of knowledge or because they are already "slim," but these athletes don't realize how much potential they are wasting.

The intensity-duration profile

This concept was first introduced to me by a great track and field coach named Daniel Mercier. He would make different running tests at 100 percent speed on different distances on different days. He used the results (time) for each distance and transferred them using a complicated formula (Di Prampero formula, which mathematically quantifies the acceleration phase of sprinting) to find the average power calculated in Watts on each distance. He used this unit to compare athletes with different bodyweights. He then used every result in Watts to create a graph that would represent an intensity duration profile for each athlete. This intensity duration curve gives a good indication of whether the athlete is mostly fast-twitch or slow-twitch muscle fibre dominant, and to what extent.

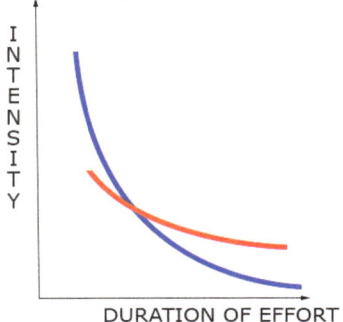

TWO DIFFERENT INTENSITY DURATION PROFILES

The athlete with the steepest curve (blue) is the one with fast-twitch muscle fibre dominance. His intensity is very high, but he can't maintain it for very long; fast-twitch muscle fibres fatigue very quickly. On the other hand, the athlete with a flatter curve (red) has more endurance but is less explosive.

At Volleyball Canada, we test athletes on single jumps with jump mats and Vertec. The myotest device is more recent, but we still use the jump mat, because all of our previous stats are with the jump mat (we want consistency in the results) and because the results of both devices are significantly different. (Furthermore, I'm not a big fan of myotest because the device often falls from the velcro belt when we test.)

The counter movement jump (CMJ) on the jump mat or the block motion jump on the Vertec – without any prior step – are excellent indicators of maximal strength, explosive strength, and arm action efficiency. The attack motion jump on Vertec is a great indicator of explosive, reactive strength and biomechanical efficiency to transfer horizontal speed to vertical speed with a great blocking motion of the feet. We use these tests to assess the degree of intensity that our players can reach.

If you are curious and want to view the results that we have on these tests with Canada's national men's junior and senior teams, they are included in the bonus section of this book.

For the duration-endurance component, even though we could, we don't conduct tests that consist of doing a high number of jumps. This is for several reasons. First, we try to minimize the number of jumps outside of technico-tactical training. The exception to this is when players have a technico-tactical training break. In this case, we increase the jumping volume so the mechanical stress doesn't diminish too much, to avoid injuries that could occur when they start back to technico-tactical training. We want to avoid a "detraining effect" of the structures to the mechanical stress. Second, jumping in a row for 15 jumps is far from being specific to volleyball, just like running 400 meters is far from running 80 times 5 meters for a running back in American football.

Third, we would rather find the duration aspect by integrating the technico-tactical aspect of volleyball. How do we do it? The coaching staff look at how the players evolve during numerous sets or reps in terms of jumping height and fatigue in game situations in training; we then estimate that intensity-duration curve. It is qualitative and not quantitative information and thus not 100 percent objective, but we can use it. We usually do these tests in the period two weeks after the professional season or after the end of university semester for younger players, and a few weeks before the start of the international season (World League) at the beginning of May. The whole coaching staff must evaluate a number of things simultaneously during that very short period. With these tests, we usually have athletes who stand in the middle of the curves. But if some are at the extreme of the curves, we will choose training priorities to improve either explosiveness or work capacity to aim for an acceptable curve. The coaching staff will notice the extremes very quickly on the court while practicing or playing.

DEFYING GRAVITY

PLAYING DETECTIVE

Not every method to improve vertical jump will fit every player.

Coaches and players must consider the risk-reward of strength and conditioning training. Some methods are extremely effective at improving explosiveness and reactivity and are used in programs to improve vertical jump. Does that mean we should use them with all volleyball players? Absolutely not! It depends on factors that should be analyzed through interviews or interrogations. In fact, the coach or strength coach should act like Inspector Colombo, asking a lot of questions and gathering a lot of information while being very discreet and low-profile about it, so the athlete doesn't feel like he or she is responding to an interrogation.

Important factors to consider

Here is a list of questions I ask myself to determine the risk-reward ratio of a training protocol that I would prescribe to a volleyball player. Most of the time, I get the answers by gathering information the Colombo way!

1. How much time do I have to train this player? Is it enough to have a real impact on him? I remember in May 2012, players were coming back from professional leagues and they had just two or three weeks before a series of qualifying competitions that would have led to the Olympics. Unfortunately we didn't qualify for them. Could I really improve something physically? In fact, I could only prevent injuries with structural balance work and keep their nervous system activated without creating delayed-onset muscle soreness. The team had to gain

back its game cohesion with technico-tactical training after a pro season's separation.

2. How old is the player? If she's young, is this method too risky or too advanced? Some coaches use too-advanced methods with young athletes to achieve fast results. An example to illustrate the nonsense of this procedure: if a fly bugs you, are you going to eliminate it with a flyswatter or a rifle? The answer is evident. If you use a rifle for this purpose, you might induce collateral damages. If the body adapts to advanced methods too early, and would have responded to more basic training stimulus first, what methods are you going to use when the athlete needs a more advanced method? Are you going to use the same methods? If the body adapted to them, are you then going to use the basic methods? It's likely that none of them will create much adaptation now, and the athlete will hit a plateau, because the coach used training methods that were too advanced and didn't give the proper stimulus to preserve the athlete's trainability for the future.

3. Is this strength and conditioning program too much in terms of workload when added to the psychological stress of school work, social life, pain, or other factors? What about the physical stress related to poor nutrition, lack of sleep, and the accumulation of technical and tactical training on the court? This leads to another question ...

4. Does the athlete have a lot of stress outside of the training environment – such as family and other relationships, money, nutrition, or food allergies or intolerance? All those factors combined together are creating what is called **the allostatic load**.

5. If the player is older, is the training method too risky with the history of injuries? Let's face it, the older a

PLAYING DETECTIVE

volleyball player gets, the bigger the injury history becomes, even if every recovery and postural aspect is proactively managed.

6. If the player is injured, could he or she lose a professional contract or a spot on the national team?

7. Would that affect the player's career or family? In my opinion, these three previous questions differentiate the experienced strength coach from the beginner. A coach just starting out often wants to prove his professional knowledge or worth with results – and tends to be a bit more aggressive and less conservative in the training protocol he prescribes. In volleyball, strength training is a means to an end – the goal is to be a better volleyball player. Strength training is not a goal on its own like in weightlifting, powerlifting, or crossfit.

8. What's the postural condition of the athlete? Does he have a sound structural balance or is he completely unbalanced? This can be caused by sitting too much at school, too many volleyball-specific adaptations during the professional season, or injuries incurred as a result of volleyball. Like the famous quote favored by many strength coaches says, "You can't shoot a cannon from a canoe." Another: "A Formula 1 needs to be well aligned before racing." This is why volleyball players should pay a lot of attention to their structural balance. In fact, it should be a main physical priority to remain healthy. The basis of performing well and without pain is having as many movement patterns as possible, without compensation patterns, for proper movement for training or sport performance.

9. How is the player's strength level right now? Is it enough and does it transfer well during a game? Some athletes are good players, considering their technico-tactical talents, up to a certain level. After this level,

though, they have to increase explosiveness for jumping or hitting. A lack of strength can be an issue for power development or for injury prevention with joint stability. On the other hand, some athletes are very strong but can't transfer it in power output during a game situation.

10. Is it possible that this athlete might compensate for lack of vertical jump or explosiveness with better tactical skill or experience? This last question is the toughest to ask for a strength coach who loves to improve his athletes' physical performance, but in some situations you have older experienced volleyball players where this is the case. This might happen with wise setters and liberos, and can even extend to other positions. In this case, you want them healthy and that's it.

After answering these questions, you can decide by answering this question: Do the training methods and the planning sequence in which I would use them to improve the player's explosiveness have more chances to induce adaptations that will help the player's volleyball game, or is it risky enough to negatively affect his volleyball game?

Only after answering those questions do we build the training plan.

When I was teaching training methodologies at Québec's University of Sherbrooke in the physical education and kinesiology department, I was giving my students a session paper where they had to prepare training plans for different contexts presented as scenarios. It was fascinating how some of them would use extremely good training protocols developed by well-renowned strength coaches – but the program would just not fit the context that I had presented to them. "How could this program be wrong if it was designed by coach X?" they asked. My answer was, "That coach would have probably modified the training plan by using other training protocols or by adapting them to reduce the risk-reward ratio if he had known the details of this particular context."

DEFYING GRAVITY

YOU CAN'T FIRE A CANNON FROM A CANOE!

Needed functions of joints

Physiotherapist Gray Cook invented a postural evaluation system called Functional Movement Screen[1]. Inspired by that, strength coach Mike Boyle wrote "A Joint-by-Joint Approach to Training"[2]. He explains how he perceives the body as a stack of joints, each with different needed functions. I don't adhere to the stack-of-joints model because I believe the tensegrity model[3] is closer to the way the body works, I do agree with the needs for each joint that Boyle suggests – and I would add the foot, because you can't fire a cannon from a canoe! Structural balance is critical to improving vertical jump and staying healthy on the musculoskeletal level. Here are the prerequisites for a sound structural balance:

Feet: Not too arched (supinated) and not too flat (pronated), just neutral and stable to stay healthy – see photos on the next page. However, volleyball players with supinated feet have an advantage for jumping higher. Their foot fascia, which continues to the heel and up through the calf, can accumulate more tension. Like a bow and arrow, the foot fascia and the calf would be the string of the bow and the heel would be the arrow, propelled at a 45-degree angle. I used to think that we don't have much control over the arch of the plantar

---

[1] functionalmovement.com
[2] www.strengthcoach.com/public/1282.cfm
[3] youtube.com/watch?v=BzgxYpDyO0M

fascia, a long thin ligament directly under the skin on the bottom of the foot.

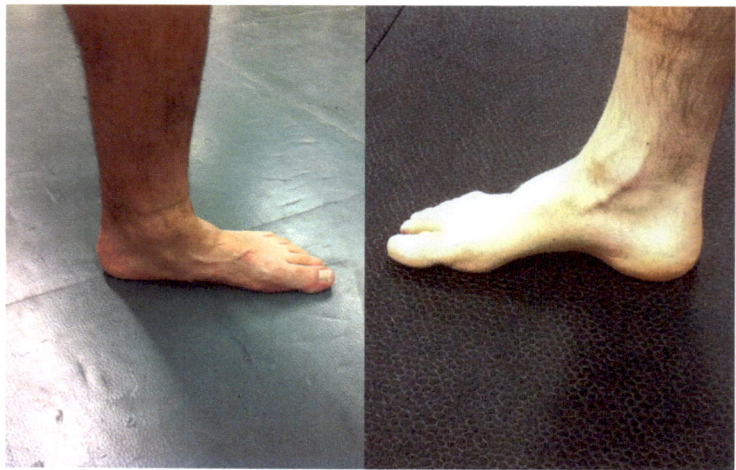

LEFT: PRONATED FOOT   RIGHT: SUPINATED FOOT

But with Thomas W. Myers' book *Anatomy Trains*[4], I'm re-evaluating my position on that topic. We might have a small incidence with adults and a moderate incidence with children on changing our foot arch. I won't cover this topic because it's beyond the scope of this book, but Myers' book explains it very well. Even if supinated feet are a biomechanical advantage for jumping, neutral feet will keep you healthier over time!

Ankles: Mobility is important in the sagittal plane (plantar flexion and especially dorsiflexion) for a good range of motion and for avoiding shin splints; stability in the frontal plane helps avoid ankle sprains.

---

[4] anatomytrains.com/at/

YOU CAN'T FIRE A CANNON FROM A CANOE

Knees need stability in the frontal plane. You want to avoid varus knees (bowed out like the right photo), often related to supinated feet, because they are very stressful for the lateral collateral ligaments and IT bands. You also want to avoid valgus knees (bowed in like the left photo), often related to flat feet. The valgus knee is stressful for the medial collateral knee ligaments.

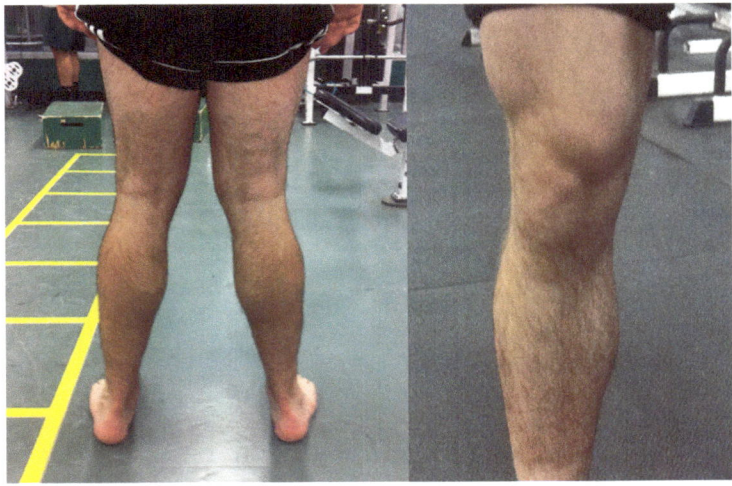

Hips: Mobility in all planes.

Lumbar spine: Stability to fight shearing forces produced from the powerful actions of the legs while jumping, to transfer this power to the arms in a summation sequence with a minimum of wasted energy. This stability is often referred to with the term core – for abdominal (transverse, quadratus lumborum, internal and external obliques, and rectus abdominis [5]) and posterior chain muscles (glutes and deep erector spinae group[6]).

Thoracic spine: Mobility in the sagittal plane, is important, especially in extension to avoid kyphosis[7].

Gleno-humeral joint (shoulder): Stability is important because the shoulder is a joint that is already very mobile and unstable. Volleyball players use them continuously and thus often have hypermobile shoulders that induce pain. Some of the posterior muscles are too weak and stretched, while some of the anterior muscles are too shortened.[8]

Each joint has different needs in an alternated sequential order. Postural problems develop when some muscles get too strong or too short and other muscles get too weak or too loose.

---

[5] ironworkout.com/ab_workout.htm
[6] eps-delataille.fr/Musculation/haut/Lombaires.htm
[7] mayoclinic.org/diseases-conditions/kyphosis/multimedia/kyphosis/img-20007874
[8] protraineronline.com/exercise/shoulder-injuries/

Common problems with volleyball players

If a volleyball player can maintain the integrity of his joints' movements in the right sequence as described above, he has great chances of remaining healthy. Most volleyball players, because of injuries or specific volleyball adaptations, tend to switch the functional aspect of their joints. What do I mean by that? Let's look at typical volleyball player cases.

Ankles' lack of dorsiflexion mobility repercussions

Most volleyball players might hurt their ankles while attacking or blocking during their playing career. What happens next? Even if it's well treated and it heals well, there will be scar tissue in the ankle's ligaments. This scar tissue has less elastin, which is the elastic material in a healthy and uninjured ligament. This situation will greatly reduce the mobility of the ankle in all planes, to avoid another sprain. While this might look like a great adaptation, if the ankle doesn't move easily in dorsiflexion while the player is playing or doing resistance training, other joints will need to compensate for that lack of mobility. The joints that are most likely to compensate for the ankle's lack of mobility are the foot (subtalar joint[9]), the knee, or the lumbar spine. These joints will create movement modifications to compensate for the lack of dorsiflexion mobility in the ankle. The foot will have a tendency to be flat or pronated.

Because of the pronation of the foot, the knee will be bowed in, which is called a valgus condition. This valgus knee action will put stress on the medial collateral

---

[9] goldenearsphysio.com/niraj-thakore/take-me-out-to-the-ball-game-subtalar-dislocation-2/

ligament, the internal meniscus, and the anterior cruciate ligament.[10]

This increased stress on theses knee structures increases the likelihood of knee pain or serious injury. The lack of mobility at the ankle might even need correction at the lumbar spine by "rounding the lower back." This will increase the likelihood of back pain.

Quadriceps and hamstrings strength discrepancies

Volleyball players also often have big discrepancies between their hamstring strength and their quadriceps strength. Because of the number of jumps and landings (which no other sport is even close to), they accumulate much more tension in the quadriceps than the medial portions of the hamstrings (semimembranosus and semitendinosus). With that condition, they accumulate tension that might create the "jumper's knee" syndrome. This phenomenon usually occurs in the opposite leg of the hitting arm, the leg on which the players are blocking first after the approach step and the one they are landing on with the most weight, most of the time when they attack. For example, a right-handed hitter will take the first step with his left leg to accumulate horizontal speed. He will then use his right leg to block the momentum and initiate the transfer in vertical pushing followed by the left leg. Once he's in flight, he will hit the ball with his right arm and will often land with his left leg touching the floor before the right one because of the torso stabilization need. So right-handed hitters have very tight

---

10 interactive-biology.com/3992/functional-anatomy-of-the-knee-movement-and-stability/

quadriceps and hamstrings on the left side and vice-versa for left-handed hitters.

Hips lack of mobility: why and repercussions

Concerning the hip joint, volleyball players have a tendency toward large lack of mobility as a result of different aspects. First, when young, these athletes' bones grow so fast that the strong muscles that pass through the hips have a hard time adapting to the change of tension resulting from the origins and insertions (points of attachment of muscles on different bone structures) that are being literally pulled away. If they don't adopt a frequent flexibility and mobility routine, these tensions will stay and even increase when athletes gain more muscle mass.

Second, these athletes are seated all day long in front of computers, like a good portion of the population, and are in a standing bent position for passing actions or acceleration during a significant portion of the game. These positions shorten hip flexor muscles like the rectus femoris and the psoas. As a result of having tight hip flexor muscles, volleyball players often have an inhibition of the glute muscles. In fact, most volleyball players that we test are very weak at the glute muscles. What do they do to compensate? Their neural system asks less powerful muscles such as the lateral portion of hamstrings (called biceps femoris), the external portion of the quadriceps, or the fascia latae to perform the tasks that require the potential power of the gluteal muscles. This condition is often the reason for low back pain, tight iliotibial bands (IT Band syndrome) and patello-femoral pain (jumper's knee). Stretching the hip flexor muscles and strengthening the gluteus maximus and the gluteus medius is helpful in fixing these problems.

Many volleyball players have low back pain because the muscles that pass through the hip joint, i.e. glutes, hamstrings, psoas, rectus femoris, pyriformis, tensor fasciae latae (which becomes the IT band at the lower portion of the thigh) are too tight. We must not assume that a tight muscle is a strong muscle, even if it's sometimes the case. A muscle might be tight *and* weak. A few muscles in that area might have both conditions. To make sure that it is the case, evaluating players is paramount. Those shortened muscles that attach to the pelvis create a lot of tension in that area. Imagine that those muscles are like chocks too tight, and flat tires, on a bicycle doing curb jumps. The frame of the bicycle (the spine in this example) is getting all the impact. This is what happens to the lumbar spine of the volleyball player who jumps with too-tight muscles around the hip joint. The hip muscles should be loose enough to have an impact in absorption. Also, the lack of mobility in the hips will be compensated for by mobility at the lumbar spine. This will result in a considerable amount of lost energy and will put stress on the lumbar spine structures that could even lead to spondylolisthesis.[11]

Lumbo-pelvic stability

Lumbo-pelvic stability, better known as core, is essential in transferring the power from lower extremities to upper extremities with a minimal energy waste and a minimal stress on the lumbar spine. If muscles such as transverse, internal and external obliques, quadratus

---

[11] emedicine.medscape.com/article/396016-overview

lumborum, and the rectus abdominis are weak, the chances of low back pain are increased. The priority function of these muscles should be torso stability over torso mobility – but both are important. This is why the crunch exercise, a torso flexion (torso mobility), and its derivatives are not very popular in testing abdominal strength with our team and with many other strength coaches. Because volleyball is a sport of intensity, these muscles are, in my opinion, very well trained in strength with short-duration sets (short time under tension).

Some people will argue that because these muscles are postural muscles, we should train them in endurance. While I agree with this statement, especially if core is really weak, we must remember that volleyball's main demand on abdominal muscles is stabilizing the torso, transferring and adding power from the lower body to the upper body. Doing core in endurance can be beneficial, but too much of it might create general fatigue and hip flexor muscle tension, and not train the abdominal muscles to transfer lots of power. Volleyball players need a minimum of basic "core" trained with low intensity and endurance work because they are tall, but once this is acquired, they also need to stabilize their torso and transfer lots of power. The sport by nature is very demanding on abdominals, so the training load must be well monitored. Also, using compound exercises (multi-joint movement exercises such as squat, deadlifts, etc.) in maximal strength or explosive strength will already train the core by integration because of the nature of these movements. In the programs I prepare for volleyball players, the direct localized abdominal work is limited in volume, but the degree of tension is moderate to high if the player is ready for it. Core also includes torso and pelvis stabilization by the glutes and back extensor muscles. These muscles, especially glutes, are often even weaker in proportion. This is why I also work on targeting these muscles for "core" stability. Finally, some volleyball players have weak abdominals because they move their torsos to compensate for their lack of hip mobility. Hip mobility work, therefore, should be part of the equation to improve the core.

Here is a text written by Christian Thibaudeau on how the core should be trained. I used to be a high-intensity proponent, but I'm now much more moderate in my opinion.

High rep proponents: These individuals make the argument that abs, being postural muscles, are predominantly slow twitch. As a result, they'd be better suited for work of long duration at a low intensity. High rep proponents also argue that since the ab muscles are activated almost all day long, they're built to handle a lot of training volume. Most of the time they recommend performing unloaded (non-weighted) sets of basic ab exercises, generally doing at least 15 reps per set and sometimes up to 50-plus reps.

Low reps with added resistance proponents: According to this school of thought, muscle tissue is muscle tissue. The abs are no different than any other muscle group in the body and should be trained accordingly. This group sneers at the supposed slow twitch dominance of the abs, arguing that even slow twitch fibers have the potential to hypertrophy and should still be trained in a hypertrophy-friendly zone. Their recommendation is to train the abs just like any other muscle group: if you want more abdominal definition you must hypertrophy them, and that requires work in the 6-12 rep range with added resistance.

The Verdict: Both camps have valid arguments. It's true that muscle tissue is muscle tissue and if you want to hypertrophy your abs, you must respect the overload principle. At some point that'll require using added resistance.

A lot of people cringe when they hear "abs" and "hypertrophy" in the same sentence: they think that this necessarily means making their waist thick and blocky. Not so! In fact, if you want maximum abdominal definition, you must hypertrophy them. That's what will cause the contrast between the muscle bellies and the linea alba, which will give you that six-pack look.

On the other hand, EMG research has shown that unloaded exercises such as the crunch, reverse crunch, V-sit, and crunch with a twist all activate the ab muscles to at least 60% of their maximum capacity, with a high point of 75% for some exercises. This is a sufficient hypertrophy threshold for beginners and even for intermediate trainees.

The verdict is that both types of work (loaded and unloaded) should be part of your ab training program. With loaded exercises you should train in the upper portion of the hypertrophy zone which is 10-12 reps. Beginners should use mostly unloaded slow movements and intermediates should use an equal mix of both. Finally, advanced trainees should use a ratio of two loaded exercises for one unloaded exercise.

Shoulder issues

The gleno humeral joint (shoulder) is very mobile. This joint is the connection of the humerus (arm bone) in the glenoid cavity of the shoulder blade (scapula). Because of its high mobility, it must be primarily stabilized by muscles to avoid shoulder pain. If shoulder ligaments become prime stabilizers as a result of muscle imbalances, ligaments are likely to be strained, causing shoulder pain for the player. The gleno humeral joint's condition in terms of stability and mobility is influenced by the scapulo thoracic joint, which is the shoulder blade position on the thoracic cage. Volleyball players have a tendency toward rounded forward shoulders because of their morphology, but also because of the passing positioning. This position pulls the shoulder blades apart, called protraction. This accentuates the rounded curve of the thoracic spine, called kyphosis, and can shorten the anterior muscles that pass through the shoulder joint, including the pectoralis major, the pectoralis minor, and the anterior deltoid. This condition often creates limitation or pain at the shoulder joint during explosive actions. We use exercises to help volleyball players get the stability required for a better structural balance; the book *Stretch to Win*[12] offers great tools.

Postural analysis to prevent injuries

This book is not about assessing and correcting posture – that would require an entire book of its own. The goal of this chapter is more about awareness of posture's prerequisite for explosiveness and health, which should come along together for a long and pleasant volleyball career. Some coaches or athletes might think that this is the responsibility of physiotherapists, kinesitherapists, or other manual therapist practitioners, but a lot of this work should be done early as "prehabilitation" work rather than rehabilitation – when

---

[12] amazon.com/dp/0736055290/

it's sometimes too late. For more information on assessing and correcting posture or creating an individualized strength program for a postural condition, there are numerous resources that cover the topic in detail. In the bonus section of this book are links to books and workshops that will help you deal effectively with that aspect of the volleyball player's physical prerequisites to health.

DEFYING GRAVITY

STABILIZE THE CANOE WITH 22 GREAT PILLARS!

Amount of force

A volleyball player's jump height depends on the amount of force he can apply to the ground at the short period of the takeoff. "The height of your jump depends on the vertical velocity of your center of gravity at takeoff," wrote Thomas Kurz in *Sports Skills and Strength Training*. "The greater the force and the longer the time that force acts on your body, the greater that velocity and the higher the jump. The only way to extend the time the force has for acting is to increase the distance the center of gravity travels, so there is more time for acceleration."[13]

Kurz explained that human anatomy limits the method's effectiveness because lowering the center of gravity requires bending the knees; bending them below 140 degrees reduces the efficiency of the leg muscles. This leaves just one option: increasing the athlete's force by making the leg muscles stronger.

An epic debate about the topic

Does that mean that the athlete should strengthen his legs only from a range of motion of 140 degrees of flexion and above? While some coaches think so and debate about it, I don't agree with this philosophy. Let's take squats for example. When I was in Europe with Volleyball Canada, I saw players doing quarter squats that might be

---

[13] www.stadion.com/sports-skills-and-strength-training-part-ii/

based on the 140-degree of knee flexion biomechanical efficiency theory or the fear of having too much muscle soreness for technico-tactical training. Playing and practicing in pro league with a crazy schedule doesn't leave much room for muscle soreness. However, if the volleyball player has the right postural prerequisites necessary for a full range of motion squat, and if he has the proper training and recovery context, it will produce much greater results on his vertical jump than partial range of motion squats would. A 2012 study, *Influence of Squatting Depth on Jumping Performance* [14], clearly proved it. One of the hypotheses for this is that the glutes and hamstrings contribute a lot in the jumping, and they are trained more adequately in the full range of motion squat than in partial range squats. Another hypothesis of mine is that full flexion in full squats will stimulate better the vastus medialis obliquus (VMO) muscle than the partial range squats that help the vertical jump height.

Why preventing ACL injuries is so unpopular

The VMO is the medial part of the quadriceps, and it's extremely important for vertical jump because of its stabilization role in preventing knee injuries – but also in transferring power. It is mainly stimulated in three different situations:

- when the knee is fully flexed and the patella (knee cap) is above the toes,
- when the knee is fully extended or hyperextended like at the end of the push-off of a jump motion
- when the leg or the foot is slightly externally rotated.

---

[14] www.ncbi.nlm.nih.gov/pubmed/22344055

The problem is that all these conditions are almost never met in the gym because we hear too often some key elements like "don't go too deep, it's dangerous, be careful so that your knees don't go beyond your toes because it will put too much tension in your quadriceps tendons, don't hyperextend your knees not to stress the posterior cruciate ligaments, don't do an external rotation of your feet" and so on. While some of these statements might be true in some cases, applying them blindly to all individuals and in all situations avoids VMO stimulation, resulting in weaker VMO and causing a higher risk of ACL injury through less knee stabilization. This is even truer for women because a woman's Q angle is higher considering her wider pelvis. The Q angle is the angle that the line of the rectus femoris (the muscle of the quadriceps that starts on the pelvis and attaches to the tibia by attaching first to the patella) forms with the patella. No wonder there are so many ACL tears for women in sports.

22 great exercises for structural balance

Structural balance is always a prerequisite to developing strength and power to improve vertical jump or explosiveness on the court. Here's a good story to illustrate this statement. A volleyball coach once told me that he had a very bad experience with a strength coach who had a background in track and field. I was curious because I had just told him that this was my background. I asked him what the problem was. He replied that the strength coach he worked with always wanted to do maximal strength or power exercises with very high intensities. He wanted to do low repetitions exercises with heavy loads. The volleyball coach was concerned about injuries risk and asked if the strength coach could start with less intense exercises as a preparation. The strength coach replied that this wouldn't be an effective way to improve vertical jump and that the program would be ineffective. They stopped working together.

In this story, both coaches were right. The strength coach was correct in that structural balance work won't directly improve explosiveness in a significant manner – but it will align the body to be ready for that kind of work, to be more effective and less risky. On the other hand, his unwillingness to wait for this cycle and start with structural exercise tells me a lot about his work. He either didn't know about it or he was just in a hurry to show fast results to prove his professional worth. In either case, he was about to build a card castle.

When structural balance is attained to a certain acceptable degree, then maximal strength, explosive strength, and reactive strength can be developed safely and effectively in later cycles. The exercises that I present here are mostly considered auxiliary exercises because their metabolic cost is lower than big compound exercises such as squats or deadlifts. This means that many of these exercises should be scheduled later in the sequential order of a program including primary exercises that develop maximal strength, explosive strength, or reactive strength – because their metabolic cost is less. However, in a structural balance cycle, these exercises should be considered primary exercises. Let's look at a few exercises that I consider well-suited to that purpose.

Split squat

The key points are:

- Have a straight torso throughout the whole execution.
- The hamstring of the front leg touches the calf of the front leg.
- The knee is aligned with the toes and should go near or above the toes depending on the levers of the player, because the movement is a forward translation to stimulate the vastus medialis obliquus.
- The heel of the front foot should always touch the floor.
- The knee of the rear leg should be behind its hip to stretch the hip flexor muscles.

This exercise will strengthen the VMO of the front leg to stabilize the knee, and it will stretch the hip flexor muscles of the rear leg.

Step-ups

- The height of the step should be at mid-shin or lower
- Keep a straight torso all the time. If you lean forward, the glutes will do the work, this is not what you want for this exercise, because you want to use it to stabilize your knee.
- The knee of the front leg should be aligned with the toes.
- The rear leg should be extended during the whole exercise to be passive. The heel of the rear leg should be in contact with the floor and the toes should be elevated to avoid pushing with the toes and thus "cheating."

Poliquin step-ups

The main points:

- Use a step that is at ankle height to start.
- The heel of the foot on the step must be elevated with a plate or a slant board.
- The weight should be on the ball of the elevated foot and there should be minimal or no weight on the heel of this foot.

- The heel of the leg on the floor should be placed beside the ball of the foot elevated. Thus the knee of the elevated leg will surely be above the toes.
- The free leg should touch the floor only with the heel and should remain free for the whole range of motion except when the heel touches the floor. The only leg that touches the step is the one on the step.
- The torso must stay upright during the exercise so the VMO is stimulated and not the glutes.

- If you have no resistance, you should put your hands stuck on your pelvis to avoid stabilizing yourself with your arms. You want the VMO to do the stabilization work.

This exercise was invented by strength coach Charles Poliquin as a progression toward the more difficult Petersen step-ups.

Petersen step-ups

- This is similar to the Poliquin step-ups, but tougher.
- In this exercise, the athlete doesn't have support with a plate or a slant board at the elevated heel on the step.

- He has to elevate the heel by pushing the knee forward and keep it this way during the step-up motion (concentric phase).
- The weight should be on the ball of the elevated foot and there should be no weight on the elevated

heel during the step-up motion. Once the leg at the bottom of the step is pushed to the same height as the one on the step, the heel of the leg on the step can be put on the step.
- If the athlete has enough balance, the free leg never touches the step.
- The athlete will have to elevate the heel of the leg on the step by pushing the knee forward before lowering the free leg to put an eccentric overload on the VMO.

This exercise is probably one of the best exercises to stimulate the VMO but the knees must be healthy to use it. In my experience, you can't do it for too long (more than a month) consecutively because it is stressful for the ball of the foot and the plantar fascia.

Hip thrust

- This exercise can be done on a bench or on the floor. I prefer using the bench because the range of motion is greater and there is no problem with countering the slippering effect at the thoracic area.
- Sit beside a bench and put the weight on your heels on the floor.
- Make sure the bench is secured and that it won't slip.
- Put the bar on your pelvis. You might need a cushion because the pressure of the barbell on the pelvis is uncomfortable.
- Put your shoulderblades on the bench – but also the back of your head so your neck muscles are not contracting to maintain the position.
- Do the exercise by pushing with your heels and squeezing your glutes to elevate them. The motion

is to start with an anteversion to a retroversion pelvic tilt.

This exercise fires the glute very effectively and it stretches the hip flexor muscles such as the psoas. Many volleyball players have very weak glutes that don't fire well because they have too-tight hip flexors from remaining in a seated position for too long or because of the passing position, where the hip flexors are also tight. They compensate for their lack of glute strength by using other muscles such as the IT band, which creates hip or knee problems.

Reverse hyperextension

- Use the reverse hyperextension machine
- Contract your abdominals to stabilize your back
- Keep your knees extended as much as possible
- Squeeze the glutes to elevate the weight

- Lower slowly in control
- Make sure the lower back stays straight when you lower the weight

This exercise also stimulates the glutes and the lower back. However, this machine is not very popular in gyms, and doing it without the machine, it is more difficult to overload the movement properly.

Goodmorning

- Feet can have different width as a base of support. This variable will have an influence on the muscle fibers of the hamstrings.
- Slightly bend your knees.
- Initiate the movement by pushing the hips backward.
- Continue the hips and torso flexion until there's a lot of tension in the hamstrings.

- Do the hip extension by squeezing the glutes. The movement finishes when the torso and the legs form a 180-degree angle, not more or less.
- Make sure your lower back is neutral during the whole range of motion.

This exercise strengthens the hamstrings, the glutes, and the back extensors. It also overloads the hip extensors in a movement pattern that is very similar to jumping.

Lying leg curl

- Lie prone to the machine.
- Make sure the knee joint is beside the pivot point of the leg curl.
- Raise the legs at a 90-degree angle with a regular speed throughout the whole range of motion. Don't explode to bend the knees while they are fully extended, because the hamstrings are very strong in

that position but weaker a little later in the range of motion – this could cause a hamstring tear.
- Make sure the hips don't bend (glutes elevation) while you do the knee flexion.

- You can play with the feet placement to stimulate different parts of the hamstrings. Because the semi-membranous is often the weaker muscle of the hamstrings, you should do more reps with the feet internally rotated. Because the biceps femoris is almost always the strongest, volleyball players shouldn't do much of this exercise with the feet externally rotated.

Glute ham raise

- Brace your feet in the machine so the legs are parallel to the floor.

- Put your knees on the platform or the cushions, depending on the machine you use.
- Lower the torso slowly by extending the knees. The torso should go to the lowest point possible while keeping the whole back straight and aligned with the hips' angle.
- Come up by flexing the knees while keeping the hips fully extended.

- Squeeze the glutes to keep the hips extended during the raise. This will strengthen your glutes and it will protect your back from spasms that could occur if back extensors take all the load of raising.

This exercise strengthens the glute and the hamstrings. If you don't have the machine, you can use the natural glute ham raise, which is the same exercise performed without the machine. Do it with a partner or with a stable bar to brace the feet and do the same motion.

STABILIZE THE CANOE WITH 22 GREAT PILLARS

The focus should be on the eccentric phase (lowering) and you should help yourself with a push or with elastic attached to the torso to go up. However, most volleyball players are not strong enough to do natural glute ham raise because of long resistance leverage caused by their height. This biomechanical disadvantage needs to be taken into consideration.

Heel elevated full squat

- Elevate the heels with a slant board at the required angle or with plates of different width, depending on the lack of mobility of the ankles.
- Elbows remain under the bar at all times.
- Initiate the squat pattern by bending the knees and then pushing the glutes backward so the hamstrings touch the calf while the torso remains straight.
- The weight remains on the heels.

- The knees will probably go beyond the knees and that's all right.
- This squat is really a high bar knee dominant squat and has nothing to do with the powerlifting method.

A full squat with a straight torso is a compound exercise, but it can also have a structural balance effect even if it's a bilateral exercise. Many volleyball players can't do full squats because of a lack of ankle mobility caused by ankle sprains that put a lot of scar tissue in their ankles. I use the heel-elevated deep squat to help them go deeper so they can better use their glutes, hamstrings, and VMO muscles to jump higher. Some will say that this doesn't correct the ankle mobility; I totally agree with that, but it does the job while the ankle mobility is getting fixed. To fix the ankle mobility, our players do mostly soft tissue work and myofascial stretching. Some players just can't do deep squats because of hip joint or other biomechanical limitations. Even if we do ankle mobility, they will stick with this method of doing squats; they go as deep as possible while keeping a straight torso. Some players bend their torso so far forward to compensate that it's not really a squat anymore. You want to avoid this situation.

Hip adductors

You can do this on a Swiss ball, squeezing it as hard as you can in an isometric muscle action. You need to vary the angle of knee flexion to stimulate all the hip adductor muscles. This is a great technique, but the downside of it is that you don't get an eccentric stimulus.

The other strengthening method I use is to have the player lie on the floor with his back facing a wall, then elevate both legs with the knees extended and feet apart against the wall. The lower foot will go touch the upper foot, while the upper foot and leg will stay up. The lower leg will then lower slowly without touching the floor.

Clamshell

This exercise will stimulate different fibers of the medial glutes, depending on the hip and knee angles in flexion.

- Lie on the floor or on a mat on your hip and on your shoulder.
- Flex your hips and your knees. Variation of angles is important.
- Both feet are held together one over the other. Your feet are going to be a pivot point.
- Keep your lower back straight and make sure it remains straight during the whole execution by putting a hand on it. This way, it won't move to increase the range of motion of the hip abduction.

- Open the hip of the higher leg to separate it from the lower leg. This will activate the glute of the leg at the top. The range of motion should be limited because the lower back is straight.
- You can overload the exercise with an elastic.

Prone Y

With this exercise, I have players do them either in a bent-over position or on an incline bench press. I prefer using the incline bench press so they don't compensate by swinging the hips or the torso to generate the movement.

- Stick your forehead on the incline bench.
- Keep your elbows fully extended during the whole movement.
- Retract your shoulder blades while keeping your superior trapezius very relaxed; your shoulderblades should stick together while your collarbones should be immobilized.

DEFYING GRAVITY

- When your shoulderblades are stuck together, keep the position and start lifting your arms at a 45-degree angle to your torso. The thumbs should be pointing toward the ceiling.
- The arms should be so high that if someone looks at you from a sideview perspective, they should see your ear. If you can't clear the ears, it's okay, but it means that shoulder mobility can be improved with mobility work.
- This 45-degree arm elevation action will lower the shoulder blades (scapula depression) and thus activate inferior trapezius, which is a blessing for volleyball players' shoulder health.

Scarecrows

With this exercise, I have players do them in a bent-over position or on an incline bench press; I prefer using the incline bench press so they don't compensate by swinging the hips or the torso to generate the movement.

STABILIZE THE CANOE WITH 22 GREAT PILLARS

- Stick your forehead on the incline bench.
- Raise the arms so the elbows point at the ceiling; the forearm and the arm should form a 90-degree angle.
- While keeping the elbows elevated, make an arm's external rotation.
- When the forearms are parallel with the torso, press the dumbbells forward so the elbows are fully extended.
- The arms should be above the ears to stimulate the inferior trapezius.
- Come back from the position and repeat.

Scarecrows stimulate shoulders' external rotator muscles and inferior trapezius.

Klokov press

This exercise strengthens the inferior trapezius. It is named for the Russian weightlifter Dmitri Klokov, who was doing this with 110 kg and popularized the exercise.

- Use a bar that you put on your shoulders as if to do a back squat.
- Use a wide grip as you would do a snatch exercise.
- Do an external rotation of the arms so the elbows are going forward.
- Finally, press the bar over your head while keeping the elbows forward to lower your shoulderblades and thus activate the inferior trapezius.

Incline dumbbell biceps curl

I really like this exercise because the shoulder joint is extended, and it activates very well the long portion of the biceps brachialis, which has a great influence on arm deceleration. This will help prevent labrum injuries.

- Lie on an incline bench to extend the shoulder joint.
- Position your elbows on each side of your torso.
- Extend the wrists so the wrist flexor muscles won't assist the biceps brachialis.
- Flex the forearms to a 90-degree angle.

- Lower slowly while maintaining the wrist extension throughout the whole range of motion.

Bird dogs

Lumbopelvic stability is very important to prevent back injuries and to help transfer power from the lower body to the upper body. One of the exercises that I like is bird dogs to improve lumbopelvic stabilization and glute activation at the same time. This exercise has also the advantage of activating the inferior trapezius and doesn't put tension in hip flexor muscles. This should be one of the first exercises to master for a volleyball player.

- Lie prone on a Swiss ball, be on your knees (quadrupedy) or on your toes – depending on your strength – and stabilize your body with your hands.
- While keeping the torso and pelvis straight, raise one of your hands and the opposite leg while keeping balanced and without twisting or turning the torso or the lumbar spine.

- When it becomes easier, increase the speed of the movement in the elevation (concentric phase) while still stabilizing the pelvis and the torso.

Stir the pot

Popularized by world-renowned Canadian back pain researcher Stuart McGill, the exercise stir-the-pot is another core exercise that I like because it stabilizes the lumbopelvic area without putting too much tension in the hip flexor muscles.

- Put your forearms on a Swiss ball in a plank position.
- Stabilize the torso and the pelvis.
- Make circle motions with the arms while keeping the pelvis straight and stable.
- If you are stronger, increase the size of circles while still stabilizing the pelvis.

Reverse V-up to roll out

Even if I don't like putting too much tension in hip flexor muscles, there are some exercises that put a little bit of tension in hip flexor muscles. This one was popularized by Nick Tumminello.

- Put your feet on the Swiss ball or attach them in the power wheel (if you have one and you want to increase the difficulty level).
- Take a push-up position with a straight back and with the elbows extended.
- Flex the hips and raise the glutes toward the ceiling.
- Come back to the push-up position with elbows extended.

- Then roll backward by doing a flexion at the shoulder level as you would do a pull-over – keep the back straight.
- Do the hip flexion while doing a shoulder extension for the next repetition.

Suitcase deadlift

This exercise is great for quadratus lumborum and for forearm flexors grip strength to finish the hitting portion.

STABILIZE THE CANOE WITH 22 GREAT PILLARS

- Stand beside the bar.
- Flex the knees and keep the back straight to grab the bar.
- Grab the middle of the bar with the hand close to the bar.
- Lift the bar by pushing with the quadriceps at the knee level.
- When the bar is at knee level, extend the hips and squeeze the glutes.
- Lower the bar and repeat.

This exercise is productive, but you have to make sure the player is weak from the quadratus lumborum. Some players are weak, but some are very tight because of a lack of glute activation. You have to make sure that you *need* quadratus lumborum exercise before doing this. As stated in the previous chapter, postural assessment is always a good idea and should be a prerequisite.

Windmill

This exercise has been popularized by Russians and by kettlebell instructors; it's great to improve quadratus lumborum strength and to improve hip mobility.

- Put your feet in a capital L position with the knees slightly bent.
- Using a dumbbell or a kettlebell as a resistance, hold it over your head while always looking at it.
- Lock the elbow over the head at all times and always look at the dumbbell or the kettlebell.
- Push the hip on the side of the hand that holds the resistance and lower the torso laterally on the opposite side without bending the knees any more. This will be a great stretch for stiff muscles.
- Go touch the floor or the shin of the leg opposite the dumbbell or kettlebell.
- Come back to standing.

Like the suitcase deadlift, the value of this exercise is dependent on the needs of the player.

Wheel torso flexion

- Begin the movement by extending the hips first, then push the arms forward.
- Contract the abdominals so the back stays straight.
- Come back by pulling the sternum toward the pubis.

Mobilization exercises?

I just covered a few strengthening exercises I like to use for structural balance. Do I use mobilization exercises? Yes I do! In fact, mobilization work should be done prior to strengthening; Michol Dalcourt, the director of Institute of Motion, said "Stability without mobility creates rigidity, and rigidity is the enemy of biology." It would take a whole book or a few to cover this topic, though, so I suggest you read and study the material (books and workshops) I provide in the bonus section of this book.

ACCELERATION: A CAR WITH A BIG ENGINE AND A LIGHT FRAME

An overlooked component for volleyball players

I don't know if it's the fear of muscle soreness or the fear of bulking too much, but I've realized that in volleyball, *maximal strength* is still often overlooked in many programs in Canada and in other countries. In fact, it is the foundation of explosiveness, which is extremely important in improving vertical jump or moving faster. To improve maximal strength, three factors must be considered and improved. These factors are: inter-muscular coordination, intra-muscular coordination, and the cross-sectional area.

Inter-muscular coordination

This is the ability of the athlete to use his muscles and segments in the best sequential order to move efficiently with a minimum of wasted energy and unnecessary mechanical stress for the structure. Volleyball players who have good inter-muscular coordination are those who move very efficiently and make it look very easy. This high degree of efficiency will also boost work capacity and prevent injuries, because there is less wasted energy from wrong movement patterns.

A good inter-muscular coordination or "movement literacy" is best learned at an early age because of the plasticity of the nervous system. Kids learn to speak another language much faster because of the same plasticity of the nervous system. Unfortunately, a lot of kids are being coached without properly learning the technical basics. To improve vertical jump the inter-muscular coordination applies mostly to concepts such as using properly reactive strength, triple extension, and arm action.

The intra-muscular coordination

This is the ability of the athlete to use the nervous system extremely effectively to produce a very high level of strength or power. Have you ever seen an athlete who wasn't very developed in term of muscle size but who could lift much more weight or jump much higher than other athletes who looked much stronger? Probably you were looking at just the appearance of their morphology. This is a good example of an athlete with excellent intra-muscular coordination. This athlete excels at producing electricity with his brain and distributing it to his fascias and muscles through his spinal cord. Many training protocols don't focus on the subtleties of what affects the workload to improve intramuscular coordination. This is an art and a science because it is all about nervous system programming (brain, spinal cord, and fascia extensibility and elasticity) to improve its efficiency. It is not only about stimulating muscles, like many training protocols advertised to put people in shape.

The training that will improve your intramuscular coordination will do three things; first, it will increase the number of muscle fibers that you can recruit by sending more electricity from your brain to your muscles to activate bigger and stronger muscle fibers called motorunits. Second, it will train your nervous system to synchronize the recruitment of these muscle fibers from

A BIG ENGINE AND A LIGHT FRAME

the smallest to the biggest so they can all contract and produce strength and power at the same time. Third, it will decrease the sensitivity of protective muscle inhibitors such as golgi tendon organs that shut down the muscle when there is too much tension. Those adaptations are great, but the coach and athletes must be aware that the more the athlete possesses intramuscular coordination, the more he needs a proper warm-up before training at high intensity; his protective mechanisms are less effective to generate more intensity.

The cross-sectional area

The third factor affecting strength is the cross-sectional area of muscles. Imagine that you would cut a muscle perpendicular to its longitudinal axis in two parts, at the exact location of its bigger diameter, and that you would measure the area in square centimeters or inches. All other parameters being equal (inter-muscular and intra-muscular coordination), the athlete with the bigger cross-sectional area will be stronger in absolute strength but not necessarily in relative strength – the strength compared with the body weight. Some coaches are reluctant to use hypertrophy phases in volleyball because they worry that the athlete gains too much mass and loses relative strength and acceleration. While this concern is totally understandable, hypertrophy (if done properly and at the right period) will help volleyball players increase their strength and diminish their risk of injuries by preparing the soft tissues to handle more tension to increase intra-muscular coordination. However, these benefits apply mostly to ectomorphic (tall and skinny) players. Mesomorphic (massive) players should be careful with the level of muscle hypertrophy they develop.

They should be aware of their body composition to avoid losing explosiveness, reactivity, and acceleration. We must not forget that acceleration equals strength divided by body mass. You want to build a car that has a big engine but a light frame, to accelerate better and defy gravity! All players have an optimal weight at which they are more explosive. Beyond this weight, even if it's muscle, they won't perform as well.

Hypertrophy for volleyball players

If a volleyball player needs to gain hypertrophy to improve the cross-sectional area, he must do it properly. There are mainly two ways to induce hypertrophy. One of them is to increase the ratio of muscle breakdown by using a good intensity weight (usually 6 to 10 RM) that you can lift long enough to create micro muscle tears that will stimulate muscle growth. The weight needs to be submaximal or near maximal. This rep range might be extended – it's not like martial law! If you take too much weight or resistance (intensity between 1 and 5 RM), the duration of the set, time under tension or the number of repetitions, might be too short to optimize the hypertrophy stimulus. I use the word "might" because it can work very well with fast-twitch muscle fiber dominant athletes who have many years of weight-training experience. Depending on the intensity-duration profile of the volleyball player, he will need to use different repetition ranges to induce this type of hypertrophy. Fast-twitch muscle fiber athletes will have hypertrophy results with fewer repetitions than others with a smaller proportion of fast-twitch muscle fiber. This is because their percentage of resistance compared with their 1 RM (100 percent) will decrease faster as the number of repetitions increases compared with more mixed-fiber profile players. This happens because fast-twitch muscle fibers are white – they don't contain myoglobin, which increases the endurance of muscle fibers. So the number of repetitions for hypertrophy results depends on which player is doing the training protocol.

The rest periods need to be short so the density is high to moderate. The rest period will vary depending on the strength level of the athlete, his size, and the metabolic cost of the exercise. The stronger and heavier an athlete is, the more break time he will need. Because volleyball players shouldn't be that heavy, breaks between 30 and 90 seconds should be fine for hypertrophy, depending on the metabolic cost of the exercise performed. For example, a deadlift or a full squat won't necessitate the same rest as a step-up exercise because they have a much higher metabolic cost. The exercises used for hypertrophy protocols are either auxiliary exercises presented in the previous chapter or primary exercises that will be presented next.

The type of hypertrophy that will result from the parameters presented above is called contractile hypertrophy. This hypertrophy has a great transfer for maximal strength and explosive strength.

Hypertrophy will also help improve vertical jump if the player gains hypertrophy at the upper body. While this statement might seem awkward because the legs push to jump, the center of mass of the athlete will increase in height if the athlete gains more weight at the upper body than at the lower body. A higher center of mass for the same player will help to jump higher. Don't get me wrong, I don't advocate training only upper body and avoiding legs so the athlete would look like a pogo –

that would be foolish. However, I often make longer hypertrophy phases for the upper body while training the lower body with intensification work (maximal strength, explosive strength, or reactive strength).

Hypertrophy less useful for volleyball players

The other way to induce hypertrophy is to have a longer time under tension (duration of the set) with a smaller resistance (usually 12 to 25 RM) to provoke a hypoxic (no oxygen) environment and to increase the oedema in the muscle caused by intra-muscular pressure for a long duration. Using this stimulus will induce sarcoplasmic hypertrophy, which is an adaptation that results in an increase of intra-muscular fluid. The contractile elements of the muscle (actin and myosin) don't increase as much in size because the hypertrophy is not stimulated by the ratio of protein breakdown per unit of time, but more by depletion of glycogen and hypoxic environment. This hypertrophy is much less useful for volleyball players because it increases the body weight without having significant gains in strength. Doing reps of 12 RM or higher is not bad though. It's very good to improve inter-muscular coordination for volleyball players, especially younger players who learn to do weight training. It can also be used in an accumulation phase to increase work capacity, or to deload the nervous system and the joints in a structural balance phase. In that case, it should be a small portion of the total physical work of the player in a global training process (season, year, etc.).

By the way, whatever the muscle fiber type dominance of the players and the number of repetitions they use, they will need to eat enough good calories to induce hypertrophy. Notice that I use the word good, because a calorie of pizza doesn't equal a calorie of broccoli or turkey.

Maximal strength for vertical jump improvement

As strength coach Ian King wrote, "The potential changes to a body from strength training with higher loads are so powerful (both positive and negative) that most people are not qualified to do it. It's like giving a kid the key to a Ferrari. They are not ready yet! First get your body ready; once you've managed this, go ahead and load as much as you want."[15] When the player has a good structural balance and his muscle mass is sufficient to withstand more intensive work, then it's time to gain maximal strength with primary exercises !

Here are the primary exercises that I use for maximal strength development for volleyball players.

Squat (front and back)

I use knee-dominant squats. Narrow stance will target the quads while wider stance will target the glutes.

You start the movement by placing the bar just under the seventh cervical vertebra on the upper trapezius muscles for back squat – this is where there's an uncomfortable bump! You want the bar under that area so it's comfortable. Elbows should be under the bar at all times when you perform a back squat. You place the bar on the front deltoids touching the throat with high elbows when doing a front squat.

---

[15] facebook.com/permalink.php?story_fbid=10151870466589036&id=352442794035

Initiate the movement by bending the knees. Then push the glutes back and go deep so the hamstrings go touch the calves and the torso remains straight during the whole range of motion. If you can't go that deep, go as deep as possible while keeping a straight torso. If the torso leans forward, I suggest elevating the heels of regular shoes – but not higher than a weightlifting wooden heel shoe. The feet can be hip width apart (or wider or narrower) depending on which muscle groups you most want to target. A narrow stance will target more the quadriceps but it will require more ankle mobility.

Deadlift

With deadlift, I use pronated grip deadlift for numerous reasons. This grip is much tougher for forearms, so it will strengthen them. Also, I like to use pronated grip to avoid biceps tears on the side of the supinated forearm of a mixed grip. Finally, the pronated grip helps prevent a too-large discrepancy of internal and external rotation of the arm because of the favorite alternated deadlift grip that will be used more often than its opposite side of the mixed grip. Dave Marois, a colleague of mine, realized that too much mixed grip created an internal and external rotation discrepancy pattern between the two shoulders. This discrepancy is affecting passing skills, either for service reception or for defending, by affecting arm and forearm placement. He learned this while following an introductory volleyball course at University for his kinesiology degree. Dave Marois was training for strongman events and had just about nothing in common with volleyball players. However, when he was trying to do passing in his class, he just couldn't do it because of his high training volume with mixed-grip deadlift for his sport.

In both cases, squat and deadlift, varying the stance in terms of feet width will stimulate different muscle groups by putting the mechanical stress on different joints.

Alternated Reverse Lunges

I know that a few strength coaches don't like to overload lunges because they cause a certain stress to the pelvis; one hip flexor is shortened and one is extended, and they put tension in the knee of the front leg. While I partly agree with this, I like overloading reverse lunges for a short period (mesocycle of 2 to 3 weeks of duration) because of the payoff in hip extensors strength for acceleration. The alternated reverse lunge is a closed chain kinetic unilateral hip extension exercise exactly like the push-off of a stride to accelerate forward on the court!

The inconvenience with this exercise is that it induces a lot of muscle soreness in the posterior chain, especially for glutes and hamstrings.

Push press

When the athlete has the minimum prerequisite for torso stability and shoulder mobility, push press is a great exercise. The player should be able to bring his arms beside his ears without compensating by moving the torso.

While doing the concentric phase (lifting), the player uses his legs in explosive strength to create a momentum to help lift the bar or the dumbbells (concentric phase) while the torso is braced. Then the deltoids and the triceps are overloaded during the slow eccentric (lowering) phase. This exercise is also useful to train torso stability if the abdominals are strong enough. Abdominals are not always strong enough with volleyball players because they are tall and their leverages are not advantageous in strength. This exercise can be done with a barbell or with dumbbells.

Pull-ups

As an upper body relative strength development exercise, I really like this exercise to strengthen the lats, the forearm flexors (e.g. biceps and biceps brachialis), and the forearms – especially wrist flexors, which help finish the attack or the block during the volleyball game.

When the athletes are more fit, I do an overload but I also very often use Fat Gripz devices, which increase the diameter of the bar and therefore the stress and strength adaptations to wrist flexor muscles. Using this exercise with Fat Gripz requires stretching forearm flexors to avoid carpal tunnel syndrome or wrist pain resulting from too much accumulated tension.

Bench press

Bench press is useful in developing upper body maximal strength. It is not specific to any movement in volleyball. However, it activates a lot of upper body muscles and thus the nervous system in a productive way. However, volleyball players need to have good shoulderblade control as a prerequisite to do bench press to avoid more risk and less benefit of doing this exercise.

Dips

Dips on V bars are great to activate triceps and pectoral muscles while maintaining a good relative strength level (strength compared with body weight). I prefer V bars because it is easier to adapt to different arms and lever lengths.

Norms for strength ratios

If the athlete is weak, which is often the case with volleyball players because of their long levers, improving maximal strength will help improve explosivity such as diving, jumping, or hitting. What is considered weak? It depends on the age of the athlete. In my experience, if a varsity level player can't manage to squat 1.5 times his bodyweight in a full range of motion for at least 3 repetitions (regardless of the reason, which is either bad posture or lack of strength), he can surely be considered weak. According to strength coach Charles Poliquin[16],

---

[16] www.poliquingroup.com

using the back squat as the reference norm, we get the following ratios:

Back squat 100 percent
Front squat 85 percent
Clean grip deadlift 113 percent

After working with structural balance, gaining experience and developing inter-muscular coordination with strength endurance and hypertrophy methods for a good strength training foundation, it's time to develop maximal strength. I use maximal strength development protocols such as conventional maximal strength protocol, cluster method, maximal isometric method, and supra-maximal eccentric efforts method.

Conventional maximal strength protocol

The athlete should use an intensity of 85 to 100 percent of the repetition maximum (RM). The number of repetitions per set should vary between 1 and 5 RM. The rest interval should vary between 3 and 5 minutes depending on the metabolic cost of the exercise (e.g. deadlift versus biceps curl), the intra-muscular coordination of the athlete (strength) and the size of the athlete. Bigger and stronger athletes need more rest than smaller and weaker athletes. The time under tension (duration of the set) is under 20 seconds, so the tempo of execution is slow because of the high degree of resistance, but the player doesn't intentionally slow down the concentric phase (lifting). In fact, the player tries to accelerate the weight. The number of sets will vary greatly depending on the work capacity of the athlete, but because the number of repetitions is low and you want to have enough volume to stimulate adaptations, the number of sets is usually higher than with strength

A BIG ENGINE AND A LIGHT FRAME

endurance or hypertrophy protocols. Because volleyball players have a lot of technico-tactical training, the number of sets is usually between 3 and 6 per exercise. However, this is not true for sports in which weight training is a goal in itself, such as weightlifting or powerlifting, where the volume would be much higher (5 to 12 sets per exercise). Volleyball players with large work capacity can do more than 6 sets per exercise, but it doesn't happen very often. The number of exercises per training is between 1 and 4. Depending on the athlete's work capacity to tolerate the training load, 3 to 4 sessions per week is okay during pre-season work, while 2 to 3 sessions per week is okay during competition phase.

Cluster method

The cluster method, also known as the rest-pause method, is useful for strength gains and is recommended if the volleyball player has completed a considerable volume with the conventional maximal strength protocol; it further stimulates the nervous system by reaching a higher intensity (approximately 5 percent higher than the conventional method). I wouldn't use this method to start maximal strength training, because such training is quite challenging and advanced. This is also useful in overcoming plateaus to increase intramuscular coordination, and I wouldn't want to "waste" the adaptations of this method when the trainability (potential for improvement) of the player is high enough that the conventional maximal strength protocol would bring great results.

Here's how we use this method. The athlete should use an intensity of 85 to 100 percent of the repetition maximum (RM). The number of repetitions per set should vary between 3 and 5. The number of sets per exercise should be between 3 and 5. The rest between the repetitions (intra-set rest) is 10 to 15 seconds. According to certain coaches, only the higher percentage of fast-twitch muscle fiber athletes should take 15 seconds of rest between their repetitions, because their muscle fibers don't contain myoglobin, which helps recovery. Keeping track of the intra-set rest and the number of repetitions performed is sometimes difficult because of fatigue. For this reason, the player should do it with a partner or a coach. The rest between sets should be between 4 and 5 minutes because it is more demanding than the conventional strength protocol. For example, if an athlete usually does 5 RM with 85 percent of his 1 RM, he would use 90 percent of his 1 RM and do 5 reps with a 10-second passive pause between each repetition. This method is effective to accumulate volume at a higher intensity.

The cluster method can be done with sets higher than 5 repetitions – even 10 repetitions. In this phase, this will bring good gains in contractile hypertrophy and thus in strength, because of the bigger cross-sectional area and better intra-muscular coordination.

Maximal isometric

Maximal isometric training is the action of generating force without movement occurring. There are two types of isometric training: overcoming isometric and yielding isometric. Overcoming isometric is pushing or pulling against an immovable resistance. Pushing against pins in a rack is a good example of overcoming isometric. Yielding isometric is holding a resistance (weight) with the objective of preventing it from going down.

Maximal isometric can be done in two different ways: maximal duration isometric and maximal intensity isometric. Maximal duration isometric is used for sarcoplasmic and contractile hypertrophy gains, depending on the duration of the contraction. Maximal intensity isometric, the one I want to focus on, is good for improving maximal strength at the joint angle being worked. According to Kurz, there's a transfer of 10 to 50 percent of the strength gained in a 20-degree range (working angle +/- 20 degrees).

Here is how we use the maximal intensity isometric method with the players of Volleyball Canada. I more often use the overcoming isometric, and I use these parameters:

Number of sets: 3 to 6
Number of repetitions: 1
Duration of effort: 5 seconds
Intensity: 100 percent (maximal voluntary effort)
Rest between sets: 2 minutes

We usually do a contrast with an exercise in speed strength when we use this method. This brings movement in other degrees of the range of motion, and we use the activation of the central nervous system to perform better with the speed strength exercise.

Supramaximal eccentric overload

This is the action of lowering or yielding in a controlled manner a weight that is heavier than the 1 RM done on the exercise. This method is advanced and it should be used only with athletes who have enough physical training background to use it. With this method, athletes can use weights as intense as 120 to 140 percent of their 1 RM because the muscle fibers are slowly stretching. This method activates big fast-twitch muscle fibers and gains a lot of strength. However, this method has a higher risk-reward ratio and it creates a lot of neural fatigue for a delayed period that might extend to several weeks. Combined with other accumulated delayed training adaptations, we used this method for the preparation of weeks 12, 11, and 10 before the 2010 world championships. Volleyball players were doing numerous sets of single repetitions and they had to lower the weight in 10 seconds to put them on the safety pins.

It worked very well. Some coaches use weight releasers at both ends of the bar to unload the bar when they touch the ground to do a concentric action to overcome the now-lighter resistance after doing the overloaded lowering portion. While this might be interesting, I don't do it often with volleyball players because of their height. They are so tall that this method becomes too risky for back injury if one of the weight releasers doesn't touch the ground while the other does.

Concentric overload

Using the concentric method overload with chains or with bands will improve the strength or the acceleration of the concentric phase of certain movements. The concentric phase is the lifting part or shortening of muscle fibers. The concept of doing a concentric overload is to overload the movement throughout the whole strength curve instead of overloading only the weakest part of it.

The strength curve is the graph of how much strength (tension) a player can create from the first to the last degree of the range of motion for a certain movement. Some exercises will have a very flat strength curve – the degree of strength won't vary much throughout the whole range of motion of the exercise. The concentric method works if the exercise to be overloaded has a bell shape strength curve, such as squats, deadlifts, or dips. Let's consider a squat for example:

At the beginning of the lifting phase, the athlete is weaker because the knees are fully flexed and the muscle fibers are fully stretched. Progressively, as the athlete squats up, his strength increases until he reaches the top of the range of motion where no more strength can be generated because the movement is done. On a regular resistance pattern, the athlete overloads the strength of only the weakest angle, which is at the bottom of the range of motion. By using chains at the extremity, the weight of the chains will touch the floor when the athlete is weaker (full flexion) and the weight of the chains will increase as the athlete is lifting and is becoming stronger.

With volleyball players, I prefer to overload the concentric phase with bands rather than with chains.

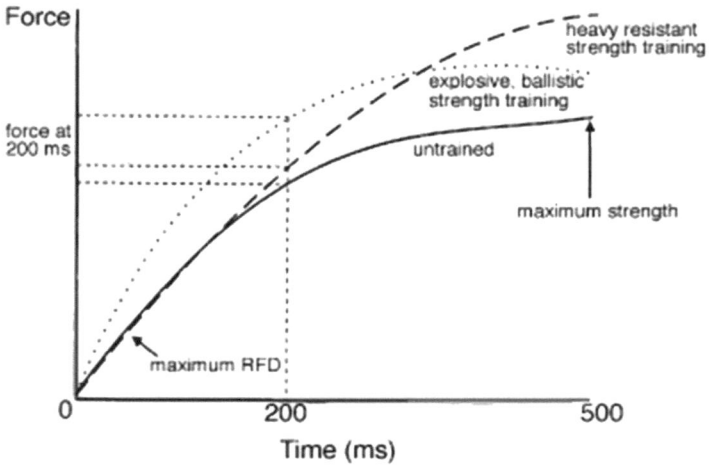

Bands force the athlete to accelerate the weight and have a positive effect on the central nervous system in learning to accelerate. With bands, if the athlete doesn't accelerate to a certain extent, he won't be able to overcome the resistance. Chains will help overload the concentric phase throughout the whole range of motion, but they might also slow down the nervous system. To have a good transfer from strength to power, you have to develop strength that will keep your strength-to-time-of-strength development ratio curve (rate of force development) as much possible to the left. Using chains might slow the rate of force development (RFD) and bring the curve to the right side.

You can attach the bands to pegs at the bottom and then on the bar at both extremities, which is what I usually do with volleyball players. With this set-up, you don't need to put much weight on the bar because the elastics are pulling down.

A BIG ENGINE AND A LIGHT FRAME

On the other hand, the coach can attach elastics to higher pegs and then attach them to the bar. This technique will help take heavier-than-usual weights in resistance because when the player squats deep, the elastics are stretched and help him pull the bar upward. As the athlete increases the range of motion, the elastics pull less and less, thus allowing the athlete to generate more force. I don't use the concentric method overload with this set-up as often, but I sometimes use it. It's good for nervous system activation and to add variety from the previous band method because of the heavier loads when standing.

Like the supra maximal eccentric overload, the concentric overload is for advanced adult athletes.

Maximal strength alone is not enough

Maximal strength is the ability to generate a maximum of force regardless of the time it takes to produce it. Improving maximal strength for weak players is a good goal. According to Thomas Kurz, though, increasing maximal strength alone is not a guaranteed way to achieve better jumping ability, because the takeoff must be kept short. You should consider how the takeoff feels for your typical jumps. Is it instantaneous and explosive, or is it sluggish? (A poor result would be 55 cm (21, 6 inches) for men and 43 cm (16, 9 inches) for women.) Poor results in a reach jump from a standstill are indicative of low explosive strength, especially if your maximal strength in a squat (measured by maximal weight lifted) is high.[17]

---

[17] Kurz, T. Science of sports training how to plan and control training for peak performance. amazon.com/Science-Sports-Training-Control-Performance/dp/0940149109

PUTTING EXPLOSIVE POWDER IN THE CANNON

What is explosive strength?

Jumping is a manifestation of explosive strength. According to Kurz's book, "Explosive strength is the ability to rapidly increase force.... It can be also defined as the ability to apply as much force as possible in the shortest time and is useful in all situations where a considerable mass has to be moved quickly." According to Professor Vladimir Zatsiorsky, it can also be referred to as "acceleration or rate of force development, or the neuromuscular system's ability to generate high action velocities."[18]

In mechanics, the formula of an impulse is force multiplied by time of application. Because of the nature of the jumping action, it usually takes between 0,12 and 0,20 seconds to do the takeoff. The best jumper is the one who can generate the most force in the most efficient way in that small bit of time.

8 EXERCISES FOR EXPLOSIVE STRENGTH

Barbell front or back jerk

This exercise consists of putting the bar on your back or on your shoulders like a back squat or an olympic-style front squat. The player takes a small dip (approximately 140 degrees at the knees) with the knees and the hips and

---

[18] bmsi.ru/doc/238b05d7-4332-4455-b41d-168736c8e3cd

then pushes very fast to accelerate the bar, locking it over his head while landing in a squat or a lunge position. This exercise has the advantage of monitoring whether the speed of the bar is fast enough to land with elbows locked, because the athlete shouldn't press the bar to finish the movement.

This exercise is a resisted jump that is highly effective in improving the vertical jump. It is also very useful in training torso stabilization (core) when the player catches the bar. However, this exercise requires a minimum prerequisite of torso stability to avoid lumbar injuries. Using jerk boxes will also prevent you from having to do a power clean to elevate the bar at every repetition, and will avoid using supra maximal eccentric work to lower the bar. Players just drop the bar on them so it doesn't stress the shoulders much. However, volleyball players who perform this exercise should have healthy shoulders and good shoulderblade control. If not, this exercise may increase shoulder problems because of the stress on

EXPLOSIVE POWDER IN THE CANNON

them. When in doubt, do it with dumbbells in a neutral grip, even if it's not as beneficial for explosive strength development because you can't transfer as much energy from the legs as with a barbell. Remember the questions regarding the risk-reward ratio!

I have found as an athlete that when you're healthy, the barbell back jerk is one of the best exercises for gaining vertical jump without doing specific jump training. A few years ago I jumped over a car to raise money for charity. While I don't recommend doing this, for several reasons, I did it for the cause. One of the main exercises I used during my own vertical jump training was the barbell back jerk.

Snatch grip jump squat

The snatch grip jump squat consists of taking the bar in a snatch grip, bending forward, and then jumping as high as possible while keeping the bar stuck to the body.

This jump squat is great because there's no risk of having the bar bouncing back on the shoulders like in a regular back squat position. It helps use the legs and the lower back muscles to develop power. This exercise doesn't work very well for numerous jumps in a short duration time to develop reactive strength (muscle extensibility and elasticity).

Hang power clean

The hang power clean is excellent for developing explosive strength.

The player starts the movement above the knee, making the force production's angle more specific while simplifying the technical aspect of the movement.

Some athletes ask me why I prefer starting from hang rather than from the floor, and I use an analogy to explain my answer. Imagine two airplanes – one takes off from a long airport runway while the other takes off from a destroyer at sea. Which plane needs more power? Obviously the one starting with a shorter runway! This is the short distance of hang clean compared with full clean.

Obviously, there is also a technical component to my preference for hang cleans.

This movement is a good way to learn the triple extension (hips, knees and ankles) and offers the possibility of using more weight than the snatch because the distance is shorter. However, a lot of players can't perform this well because of lack of mobility at the lats or wrists to adopt the rack position – or they can't catch the bar very deep in front squat position because of a lack of ankle mobility caused by too many ankle sprains. In that case, doing pulls of this exercise will be just fine until the mobility is improved with soft tissue and mobility work. The hang power clean and its variations are very good for explosive strength if technical execution is efficient. To do so, the bar must be kept very close to the body. I suggest you consult a weightlifting coach or a qualified strength coach to learn this exercise. They are the best to teach weightlifting derivative exercises.

Hang power snatch

This is an excellent exercise to develop explosive strength. The player starts the movement above the knee and makes the force production's angle more specific while simplifying the technical aspect of the movement.

DEFYING GRAVITY

This helps to learn the triple extension (hips, knee and ankles) and offers the possibility of developing more speed than the hang power clean because of the distance the bar has to travel to go over the head. This exercise has a little more technical complexity than the power clean from hang and requires healthy shoulders, which is not always a given with volleyball players. Again, I suggest you consult a weightlifting coach or a qualified strength coach to learn this exercise.

Standing box jump

The standing box jump is a useful exercise to develop power and to quantify the height an athlete can reach. The player is in front of the box and jumps without accumulating any horizontal speed. This exercise requires a solid box and thick pads to protect the shins if the player misses. We don't use this exercise too often for two main reasons: 1) players jump a lot during their technico-tactical practices and games and 2) this exercise is very aggressive for the abdominal muscles. We don't want the volleyball player to strain those muscles, so we use this exercise very carefully. It is often used to create a contrast after a compound exercise lower body exercise (mostly squat or deadlift) in maximal strength.

Front leg elevated alternated jump lunge

This exercise consists of putting the front leg on a stable step or on a gymnastic plinth. The player pushes primarily with the front leg but also with the rear leg to go as high as possible. While she is in the air, she does a full circumduction of the arms to go as high as possible, or she holds the bar tight on her back so it doesn't elevate and knock her down. Then she lands smoothly with the rear leg now going on the plinth in an alternated manner. This exercise is useful in training explosive strength to have steps similar to a jumping approach, and to prestretch the posterior chain to develop power at a similar angle. The limitation of this exercise is that if the athlete jumps very high, she needs to go up and have good kinesthetic awareness combined with a broad step or plinth to make sure she doesn't land beside the step and injure herself. The athlete should always be familiar with the movement and the set-up and slowly increase the intensity of jumps.

If the set-up is inappropriate or if the player isn't confortable with the kinesthetic awareness required, we don't do it this way – we do it as a jump split squat or a resisted jump split squat on the floor. This version is also very efficient, but it doesn't prestretch the posterior chain as much as with the front foot elevated. This exercise and its variations are often used in contrast with a preceding compound exercise in maximal strength to have the benefit of the post-tetanic potention. This phenomenon is the facilitation effect in explosive movements after doing a maximal contraction, because of the central nervous system arousal.

EXPLOSIVE POWDER IN THE CANNON

Underhand throw

This exercise is not a principal exercise, but is often used in contrast with a primary exercise (compound exercise) done beforehand in maximal strength. This exercise is intended to train the volleyball player to do an efficient triple extension (hip, knee and ankles). With this exercise the athlete can develop the maximum power output and release the medicine ball as high as possible. The higher the athlete throws the ball, the higher he jumps. This is almost a perfect correlation unless the player is overweight. Another great advantage of this exercise is that the player accelerates during the whole range of motion without stopping the movement and decelerating it subconsciously to preserve his joints and avoid injuries. The deceleration in the next exercise costs a little bit of power output.

Arm swing triple extension

This exercise is not a principal exercise but is often used in contrast with a compound exercise done beforehand in maximal strength.

This exercise is intended to train the volleyball player to effectively use arm action while doing an efficient triple extension (hip, knee and ankles).

The player starts with the arms or with light dumbbells in the hands, then takes the position of the start of a jump takeoff and aggressively does a triple extension while doing the arm movement action dynamically. The player has to stop the arm action at approximately the forehead level to avoid shoulder injury. The velocity of arm action should be so high that the player feels a blood rush in the fingers. This exercise is really interesting if you can't do an underhand throw because of ceiling height limitations. Some coaches will use kettlebell swings to train triple extensions. While that is also an interesting exercise, what I like about this version is that the player has to produce arm speed and the weight is very small; it helps the player become more conscious about the importance of arm movements while jumping. The importance of using arms efficiently in vertical jump height should not be underestimated. While testing counter movement jumps (CMJ) on jump mats, we have seen differences of up to 30 percent in height between jumps with and without arms. Producing such speed with kettlebell swing would make it flip very fast and be difficult to catch, thus greatly increasing the risk-reward ratio. Players who use the proper speed of action with this exercise should feel a bloodrush at the ends of their fingers.

Guidelines for these exercises

Because of the intense nature of these exercises, the number of repetitions should be kept low (usually between 1 and 5 repetitions) and the density should be moderate to low, so the rest period should allow a complete rest. This condition will let the nervous system recover to attain good levels of intensity.

Another kind of speed strength

Whether because of my teaching experience or my tendency to be extremely conservative in the way I classify exercises or training methodologies, you might say this chapter on explosive strength is quite short – and I would agree! Why? Because I want to put the emphasis on another type of speed strength, and that is reactive strength. Some might say that some exercises in this chapter can be done to improve reactive strength – and that is correct. However, all the exercises in this chapter can also be completed by doing a pause (isometric action) at the stretched position before doing the concentric (muscle shortening) phase, which won't train reactive strength. After this isometric action, if the player does a concentric action explosively to overcome resistance, the gains in explosive strength will be good but there will be no gains in reactive strength. Let's now take a look at reactive strength.

DEFYING GRAVITY

BOUNCE BACK!

WHAT IS REACTIVE STRENGTH?

According to Athlepedia, reactive strength is "a component of speed strength defined as a concentric contraction following a rapid eccentric contraction resulting in a greater concentric force output." In fact, all plyometric actions are a manifestation of reactive strength because they involve the stretch and shortening cycle. The definition of the stretch and shortening cycle is "a combination of eccentric-concentric contractions which function by integration of the golgi tendon organs (GTO) and the muscle spindle. There are three phases in a plyometric sequence: the eccentric phase, or landing phase; the amortization phase, or transition phase; and the concentric phase, or takeoff phase."[19]

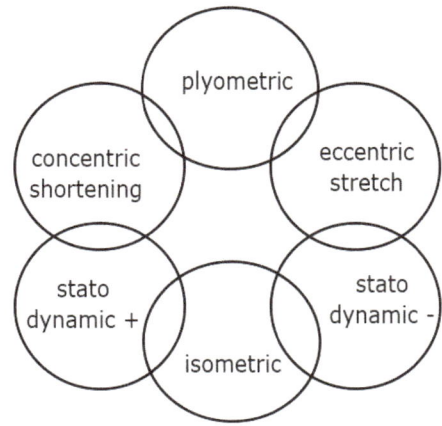

MUSCLE ACTIONS AND THEIR INFLUENCE ON POWER DEVELOPMENT METHODS

---

[19] http://athletics.wikia.com/wiki/Reactive_Strength

Consider the different muscle actions and how they relate, inspired by Jean-Pierre Egger's model in his French video, *L'héritage d'une carrière*, produced when he was training Werner Guntar. I don't use the term contraction because a contraction means a shortening and it applies only to concentric contractions. The combinations of muscle actions in the proper sequential order, at the right angle or at the right tempo of execution, can greatly improve reactive strength.

STAIRWAY TO FLY IN 6 STEPS!

To develop reactive strength, a progression for constant gains and avoiding injuries is necessary. American track and field coach Vern Gambetta[20] and French track and field coach Gilles Cometti[21] already made such a step-by-step approach with their books. I will show you a modified version that is a blend inspired by their work for volleyball context.

Step 1: Amortization phase

In this phase the volleyball player trains to land properly. He learns how to use his ankles, his knees, and his hips, and learns to align his body for an efficient amortization phase. The key points in this phase are:

- Learning how to arm the foot by doing an ankle dorsiflexion to prestretch the calves before the shortening. When I coach young athletes, I use the slingshot metaphor. I tell them they have to

---

[20] Gambetta, V. Athletic development: the art & science of functional sports conditioning. Human Kinetics, Champaign, IL: 2007.
[21] Cometti, G. La Pliométrie. Université de Bourgogne, Dijon: 1988

imagine that their feet are slingshots, their calves are the elastic of their slingshots and the ground is a bear ready to attack them. I always ask them, "Do you prefer to have your slingshot ready when the bear comes, or do you prefer to have to stretch the elastic while the bear might jump on you?" They all reply that they want to have their slingshot armed. So I tell them, "Then raise your toes but don't jump on your heels, jump on the balls of your feet."
- Learning to lean forward to stretch the posterior chain to avoid putting all the stress on the quadriceps and thus the knee joint when landing. The hips need to absorb a lot of the force.

In this training phase, the player learns how to place the body at optimal angles to learn how to land and absorb impact. The emphasis is on the silence at the ground contact. This should be taught carefully to young volleyball players, as many of them go play volleyball without learning how to land. This situation results in far more femoro-patellar syndromes compared with what would be seen had they learned how to land properly. The optimal scenario would have automated proper amortization patterns when the player is concentrating on the game! Volleyball players oftentimes have no other choice than to land on the leg opposite their hitting arm, to stabilize their center of gravity and avoid rotation. Learning to land on two legs or absorbing very efficiently on one leg is a good asset for players. Former national team captain Louis-Pierre Mainville and his coaching staff of Jump Volleyball Camps do a fine job of teaching kids how to be very efficient in this phase.

Volleyball players – and all athletes – are better trained young, because motor development that requires a lot of inter-muscular coordination is better developed when the nervous system has a lot of plasticity. Also, when athletes are young, the coach can vary body placement even if it's not the most biomechanically efficient movement. Why do this if it's not the best technique? To put variety in joint angles and in the types of jumps and landings, to minimize training monotony, to have fun and to explore what works and what doesn't work – that's why! The important thing is that the coach helps the athletes realize by themselves what works best.

This is low-impact work done in many games and drills, including playing hopscotch, leaping, jumping over low hurdles and plinths, jump ropes, and ladders. The coach has to adapt the exercise to the age and maturity of the athlete. At a young age, volleyball players are not quite volleyball players yet. *They are kids having fun* and exploring movement! A great resource for agility development is Ground Breaking 2 – a set of DVDs by a colleague of mine, Lee Taft. He is the best professional I know for agility development.

Step 2: Stabilization (landing)

In this phase, the goal is to improve the athlete's ability to stabilize after landing. The training method in this step is called negative stato dynamic. The athlete passes from an eccentric muscle action (stretching motion of muscle fibers) to an isometric muscle action (no movement in muscle fibers) by absorbing as much tension as possible with the muscles and tendons. Absorbing tension and stabilizing the body will improve reactive strength. The intensity of this method can increase to a very high level. In the context of volleyball, with the number of jumps that are so high for technico-tactical training or competition, the strength coach must assess the risk-reward ratio very carefully to include the proper components of the training load. Intensity is really the critical factor in this phase. You modulate intensity by increasing or decreasing tension. You increase or decrease tension in landing by modulating either the height from which the athlete lands or the weight of the athlete.

To increase tension, coaches will sometimes use overloads such as dumbbells, barbells, or weighted vests worn by the athlete. Those are okay as long as the player can stabilize perfectly his body with the overload and can withstand the global training load.

An example of negative stato dynamic training would be this one: the athlete does jump squat, he lands and waits for 4 seconds in isometric at a 140-degree knee flexion angle. He then jumps again with or without a counter movement (eccentric action prior to concentric action).

I don't ask mature athletes to do jump squats deeper than 140 degrees. As a coach, make sure you read the next chapter before prescribing any of these exercises, or you could cause more harm than good to your athletes.

A more advanced example to increase tension: the coach asks his players to do a depth landing from a box, keeping the landing position for 5 seconds. The coach must decide proper height for the best adaptations without unacceptable risk of injury.

Decreasing tension is easy enough by keeping the height low and lowering it, but another way to do it is to practice landings in the pool. This set-up is used mostly with rehab players, but the isokinetic (same speed of muscle action) environment of water denatures the landing motion, for an effective transfer to the volleyball court for optimal reactive strength development.

Finally, the technique we use most often is to do the stabilization and plyometric work on thick mats that absorb a lot of the impact and thus reduce stress on players' structures.

Step 3: Takeoff

In this phase, the goal is to teach or train how to improve the takeoff. In this phase, the athlete has to learn very specific points:

- Putting the feet one after the other in front of the center of gravity to transfer horizontal speed to vertical speed for takeoff. The weight rapidly shifts from heel to toe.
- Glutes pushed back to pre-stretch the posterior chain.
- Knees slightly bent not more than 140 degrees of flexion.
- Arms pulled backward to prepare to pre-stretch the arm flexor muscles (e.g. anterior deltoids, biceps brachialis).

- Flex the arm at the shoulder joint in an extremely aggressive velocity while extending in sequential order the hips, knees, and ankles to maximize the pushing action against the floor and accelerate as much as possible against gravity. While doing this, the top of the head should be pulled toward the ceiling to accentuate the extension and the movement of the center of gravity.

This takeoff step relates a lot to the exercises in the previous chapter on improving explosive strength. In fact, the takeoff is an explosive strength action that can be upgraded in power output by the kinetic energy accumulation done with the stretch and shortening cycle that requires reactive strength.

Jump takeoff phase without horizontal speed

The player might take a 4-second isometric pause down at the stretch position to dissipate kinetic energy accumulation and then explode in the concentric contraction. In this case, reactive strength wouldn't be trained at all because it's not a counter movement jump anymore (4 seconds of isometric action at the bottom), but explosive strength would still be trained.

Step 4: Standing vertical reactive jumps or fast response jumps

This step consists of doing multiple vertical jumps in a row and having a fast ground contact between them. Because the center of gravity of the athlete doesn't move horizontally, the ground contact time, or time between the eccentric and concentric muscle action (called coupling time) is reduced. A fast coupling time plyometric action is also referred to as fast response jumps. In the training process, this step is meant to learn to absorb and propel very rapidly to gain as much height as possible. This is done by jumping and landing with higher intensities. Exercises used are often hurdle jumps, standing consecutive tuck jumps, or standing ankle jumps.

Step 5: Horizontal reactive jumps or slow response jump

Because horizontal reactive jumps require a horizontal or lateral displacement at the hip joint while propelling in the concentric action, the coupling time is more than with vertical jumps; those types of jumps are called slow response jumps. Even if these jumps are called slow response, they must be done as fast as possible. In volleyball shuffle motions at the net during blocking motions can be classified in this category of jumps. Those jumps are put at step 5 because they require more stability in the amortization phase and in the takeoff phase, so they are more taxing to the torso stabilization muscles (abdominals).

In this phase, there is a progression in intensity:

- Lateral shuffle
- Leaping like running to improve hip extension in an acceleration movement pattern

In the horizontal jumps where the takeoff is with one leg and the landing is with the other, we can vary the length and the frequency of the jumps (strides). We can also bring in other types of resistance such as bands work.

- Consecutive long jumps that are very intense for abdominal work.

- Hops consist of jumping from one leg to the same leg in a leaping manner. This requires a lot of abdominal strength and a lot of leg power.

Step 6: Shock method

Also known as the depth jump or drop jump method, this is the most intense. Some athletes will jump higher using higher drop height; those athletes have a better reactive strength. It is the coach's responsibility to find the height where the coupling time is fast enough and the jump height is the highest to find the proper height of the dropping platform. Shock method should always be used with players who master the previous steps. Also, players should be perfectly healthy and have good ankle mobility. The jump volume in technico-tactical volleyball training should be lower when using this method to avoid shinsplints or other similar problems.

A few of the methods presented in this chapter might be left aside if they present more risk than benefit to your players. Every athlete is different and even international level volleyball players might stick with basic steps presented in this chapter.

CHOOSING YOUR ENEMY

IMPORTANT RESPONSIBILITY OF THE COACH

Here's an analogy I was told by a colleague named Jean Boutet. Imagine that you are in the Middle Ages and you live in a big castle with your community. One day, the castle is attacked by other people who want to kill you and take your castle. You have to fight for survival. Three scenarios might happen. First, the army attacking your castle might win and take your castle and you all die. Second, you might win easily and kill all of the others and get back to your usual life. Finally, this might be an epic battle where your community fights really hard, and the castle and the cannons are partly damaged, but you finally win over your aggressors. At the end of the epic battle, the whole community will create new towers, make new cannons, and build up the castle so that if another army arrives, you will be ready to fight them much more efficiently. As a coach, you have the power to decide which army attacks the castle. In fact, it's your responsibility and it's a very important one.

Parameters of the workload

The art of managing the external workload or the lack of details regarding this aspect will likely make or break the ability of the player to be powerful and concentrated to make actions such as jumping, hitting, and making good decisions. When preparing a training program, the coach must consider four different parameters that affect the workload: intensity, volume, density, and frequency. To induce the proper physical adaptations to the athlete, these factors must be considered as a whole. The goal is to stimulate the body into adaptations that will either improve performance or reduce the likelihood of injuries. Let's analyze separately these factors.

Intensity is related to the level of force or power that the volleyball player will produce during a movement. It can be calculated with the weight that is lifted during resistance training, the number of WATT developed during an explosive exercise – using a power-testing device such as myotest or with a height unit collected with devices such as myotest, vertec, or simply a jump mat. You increase intensity by either adding the amount of resistance (weight) when you do an exercise, or by increasing the speed of the contraction.

Volume is related to the level of training that is put into the training process. It can be calculated in different ways, such as the number of jumps, the number of sets multiplied by the number of reps multiplied by the amount of weight lifted in each rep – and finally it can simply be measured by the number of hours in the gym. When volleyball players combine technico-tactical training with strength training, the volume needs to vary to a point where the quality of the game is not too much altered. Depending on the season or the context of competition, the coaching staffs must make decisions regarding this relationship and assume the consequences on either side (volleyball or physical condition).

Density represents the amount of work as compared with the amount of rest. As an example, a training protocol with a long bout of exercises and few rest periods has a very high density. By contrast, a training protocol with short duration and high intensity exercises with long rest periods has a low density. A lot of persons in sweat qualify their training as intense when in fact it's dense. Dense training is much more painful than intense training. On the other hand, intense training requires a low density to help the nervous system rest, to better recruit the big fast-twitch muscle fibers that produce much more force and power and need a lot more of the electricity called action potential to be recruited.

Frequency represents the number of training sessions in a single week. This factor helps us see the amount of rest that the athlete has to recuperate. Frequency will vary a lot depending on the work capacity of the athlete.

WHAT INFLUENCES WORK CAPACITY?

The work capacity of the athlete, which is his ability to tolerate and recuperate from the training workload, is influenced by a lot of factors.

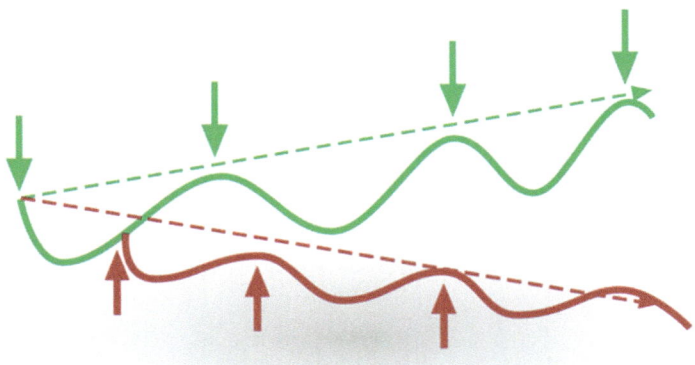

The image on the previous page illustrates proper and improper workload management with a certain degree of work capacity and the effect on performance. In this image, both curves are influenced by two scenarios: 1) different levels of workload and same work capacity of two players or 2) same level of workload and different work capacities of two players.

The factors that most influence work capacity are:
- age
- training experience
- nutrition/hydration
- mindset
- supplementation
- sleep
- genetic predisposition to tolerate any kind of stress
- manual treatments
- psychological stress
- social stress outside of the training context
- physical quality developed in comparison with the body condition

For example, for the same individual, work capacity can vary greatly in different physical qualities such as endurance strength, maximal strength, explosive strength, and metabolic adaptations. An athlete can have a great work capacity with high intensity, low density activities or exercises, such as high jump or volleyball, yet have a bad work capacity with high density and low intensity activities such as running a marathon. The opposite example is also possible: an athlete can have a great work capacity for high density and low intensity activity such as triathlon, yet have a low to average work capacity for high intensity activities such as volleyball.

Managing the workload in volleyball

In training for sports in which strength training is a goal, such as powerlifting, crossfit, or strongman, the motto is often applied: "more is better" or "no pain, no gain."

While such mottos sound great for motivation and marketing, strength training in volleyball is a means to an end – the sport – and in my opinion the motto should be: "Adequate workload matched with individual work capacity for proper adaptations." I know, it's not motivational nor good marketing, and it's too geeky – but it's what coaches should think of. If you overload the volleyball player too much too often in strength training, his technico-tactical training will suffer because of nervous system fatigue or too much delayed-onset muscle soreness. The player won't execute well technically, the decisions will be disastrous tactically, and the risks of injury will be greater. On the other hand, if you don't overload the players, they won't be trained enough to perform at their best.

For technico-physical sports that are usually practiced in solo or in small groups (e.g. track and field, powerlifting, strongmen) managing the workload with a good training plan is easier because you can calculate every set and every rep performed, the intensity (speed and resistance applied to a certain range of motion) and even the density (break time). In volleyball and other technico-tactical sports, the challenge is to monitor the whole training load of technico-tactical training added to physical training. Physical adaptations will occur by integration while doing volleyball training (technico-tactical), but to what extent?

Does any volleyball coach count the number of jumps, the height of each jump, the number of actions for each player and the time of rest they take between each action to monitor their training load? The answer is obviously no. It's simply impossible without advanced and expensive technology, especially when practicing tactical systems to train the players to make better decisions. Some coaches use feedback from athletes, but in a heterogeneous group like a team, the coach's Pygmalion effect might create a huge bias on his perception of the players' reality. According to wikipedia, the Pygmalion effect is the phenomenon whereby the greater the expectation placed upon people, the better they perform. The effect is named after the Greek myth of Pygmalion, a sculptor who fell in love with a statue he had carved. A corollary of the Pygmalion effect is the golem effect, in which low expectations lead to a decrease in performance; both effects are forms of self-fulfilling prophecy. By the Pygmalion effect, people internalize their positive labels, and those with positive labels succeed accordingly. The idea behind the Pygmalion effect is that increasing the leader's expectation of the follower's performance will result in better follower performance.[22]

With the Pygmalion effect, coaches have a tendency to overestimate the amount of fatigue for players who are tagged as "weak" in certain criteria of the coach and they'll underestimate the amount of fatigue of the players who are tagged as "strong" in these criteria. The coach's estimation is oftentimes erroneous when the player is personally assessed.

---

[22] en.wikipedia.org/wiki/Pygmalion_effect

Martin Roy, a researcher colleague of mine from Université de Sherbrooke, inspired by other researchers, developed a questionnaire for a project he did with his research team to monitor the training load and its effect on players for technico-tactical sports. While not a perfect tool because athletes need discipline, psychological maturity, and familiarization to use the tool, it was proven that it helps to monitor individual external training load better than with the coach's estimation. Denis Fontaine, who coaches women's CIS team Vert et Or of Université de Sherbrooke used that tool in collaboration with the research for the 2013-2014 season. It was proven that this tool improves efficiency to make a follow-up between the strength coach, the coaches, the players, and also the researcher's team regarding the player's level of fatigue in relation to the training load. Fonctions Optimum's team was in charge of their strength and conditioning during that research; we really enjoyed that tool.

In volleyball, the team with the best balance among technical, tactical, and physical training load to match the individual work capacity of each player has the best chances of success in the long term. This situation will prevent a lot of injuries and will help the central nervous system to be preserved for performance improvements or stabilization. For younger players, the volleyball coach may use his observations to do a "guesstimation" of the training load versus the work capacity level of the team. As players get older, using written questions to all the team members is much more precise because older players have more external parameters that influence their work capacity, and they are mature enough to communicate about them.

Next we will analyze the management of internal workload; important aspects and implications of the term work capacity will become more obvious and concrete. Remember that the motto *No pain, no gain* is not the best suited for volleyball players. Instead, the motto *Adequate workload (which relates to external workload) must be matched with individual work capacity (which refers to internal load) for proper adaptations.* Because it represents the basics of periodization, many coaches and athletes are aware of the factors influencing the external workload. However, the next chapter will bridge the gap by addressing a topic that too few coaches and players are aware of. This information is the missing link to a better performance for many athletes!

NUTRITION, HEALTH AND RECOVERY MYTHS

IMPORTANT ASPECTS AND IMPLICATIONS TOWARD WORK CAPACITY

Whenever a player has trouble tolerating the workload I prescribe, I ask questions about nutrition. Invariably, the answer is "I eat very well!"

Because a lot of volleyball players have ectomorphic morphologies (tall and skinny) and their body composition seems okay, they don't pay much attention to nutrition. Although I'm not a dietitian and nutrition can be a complicated and controversial topic, the subject is too important to be ignored.

I'd like to thank Marie-Soleil Samson, Dr. Lucie Blouin, Pierre-Luc Perreault, Dr. Jeffrey Moss, and Dr. Martin P. Albert for their assistance with this chapter.

A controversial topic

Nutrition is a controversial topic because individual metabolisms vary and the food lobbies spend a lot of money to sway opinions about what's healthy and what's not. These lobbies influence the federal government food policy committees that create Canadian food guides – as well as some dieticians. A study by Professor Norm Campbell at the University of Calgary, published in the magazine *Open Medicine*, identifies this problem with the

Canadian food guide,[23] and the organization EAT DRINK POLITICS issued a document revealing how the food industry uses sponsorships to influence dieticians.[24]

Because I've worked with many volleyball teams – some of which had dieticians – I've heard many bold statements that I disagree with, including:

- Fat is bad for athletes because it's difficult to digest, denser in calories than other macronutrients (carbohydrates and proteins), and may lead to heart disease. Therefore, your diet should be low in fat.
- Athletes NEED to eat from the four different nutrition groups (meat and protein, vegetables and fruits, grains, and dairy) to eat "well," be healthy, and satisfy their physical needs.
- Food supplements are bad because they encourage behaviours that might lead to doping. If you eat well, you shouldn't need supplements.

Are these statements true or false? The answer is: it depends. It depends on a variety of factors.

Biochemistry

To be healthy and tolerate training load, one of the main factors to consider is the biochemistry of your gastrointestinal (GI) system. Most people focus on the number of calories they consume compared with the number they burn. Few people focus on biochemistry and its effects on health and recovery. Not all calories are

---

[23] www.openmedicine.ca/article/viewFile/626/529
[24] eatdrinkpolitics.com/wp-content/uploads/AND_Corporate_Sponsorship_Report.pdf

created equal. The same number of calories from pizza won't have the same effect on your biochemistry as calories from apples. Good biochemistry leads to good metabolic health, which should be everyone's goal, especially athletes like volleyball players who need to recover from the stress of multiple training sessions.

How do we achieve good biochemistry? The first step is to reduce inflammation in the GI system.

Inflammation, diet, and health

The following information was taken from *Inflammation, Diet & Health,* by Martin P. Albert, MD and Peggy A. Wright, PhD, Med, RD from Virginia Integrative Medicine.[25] M. Albert kindly allowed me to use an excerpt from their document on food, inflammation, and the influence on health, especially on recovery from training stress.

Cleaning the mess

Inflammation is a biochemical response. Picture it as a group of people cleaning up a mess. It's okay to clean the mess, but not to destroy the walls of the house, thinking they are part of the mess. Although inflammation is an important biochemical reaction, the body can sometimes overreact, which is why anti-inflammatory medicines are so popular for acute inflammation. We often hear about acute inflammation when an athlete is injured. On the other hand, we seldom hear about chronic inflammation. This can be caused by lifestyle choices such as nutrition, sleep, or exposure to

---

25 www.healthyvim.org/Anti-inflammatory_Diet_Talk_2-26-13.pdf

pollution. Many of these choices are under the player's control, especially nutrition. By limiting inflammation, a player can improve his health and increase the amount of energy needed to perform.

Basic principle: Food is information

Foods are messengers. They talk to your genes. Do you want them to give your body a healing message or tell your body something harmful? The most valuable tool for becoming and staying healthy is your fork.

There's no such thing as junk food. Either it's food or it's junk.

WHAT'S GOOD TO EAT?

HEALTHY FATS AND NOT-SO-HEALTHY FATS

The Great:

- Extra virgin olive oil, cold pressed sesame oil, organic canola oil
- Omega 3 (cold water fish, flax seeds, walnuts, pumpkin seeds)

The Good:

- Almonds, avocados, virgin coconut oil, regular olive oil, high oleic safflower oil, nut butters

The Bad:

Too much omega-6: animal, dairy, and many vegetable oils (cottonseed, grape seed, regular safflower, corn, peanut, sunflower, soy). Omega-6 fat is linolenic acid, which creates gamma linolenic acid (GLA) and arachidonic acid (AA). In turn, these create **pro**-inflammatory prostaglandins and leukotrienes.

(Omega-3 fat is alpha-linolenic acid, which creates eicospentainoic acid (EPA) and docosahexainoic acid (DHA). These create **anti**-inflammatory prostaglandins and leukotrienes.)

The Ugly:

In foods containing artificial trans fats, up to 45 percent of the total fat may consist of trans fat. Baking shortenings contain 30 percent of fat as trans fat, and margarines may have as much as 15 percent trans fat by weight.

Fat and rancidification

For all types of fat, heat accelerates the oxidation reactions that cause it to go rancid. Rancidification alters a food's chemical structure, which affects its nutritional content and might create cancer-causing agents. Eat great and good fats, but be careful about heating them. The book *Oiling of America* by Mary G. Enig and Sally Fallon explodes many myths and preconceptions about fat consumption.

Fat, the most caloric macronutrient

Fat is the most caloric macronutrient. Carbohydrates contain four calories per gram, proteins contain four calories per gram, and fat contains nine calories per gram. Many people think that by reducing fat consumption, they will lose weight and improve their health because fat has more calories than proteins and carbohydrates. While a person needs to have a deficit between the calories input and the calories output, good biochemistry is needed to lose fat in a *healthy* way. Reducing bad fats is a great idea, but reducing good fats can be disastrous to both health and recovery from training loads.

Cell membrane health and fat consumption

Cell membranes regulate the entry and exit of certain molecules in the body. Consuming good fats, especially omega-3 in sufficient quantity, will improve biochemistry and cell membrane integrity by lowering the level of general chronic inflammation.

In integrative medicine, cell membrane health is measured by means of the phase angle (PA). At Volleyball Canada we use an RJL BIA system (a bioelectrical impedance analysis) to assess players' metabolic health. Research shows that the bigger the PA, the healthier your cells are, because cells communicate better with each other when electricity flows smoothly between them. The data we use most is presented below.

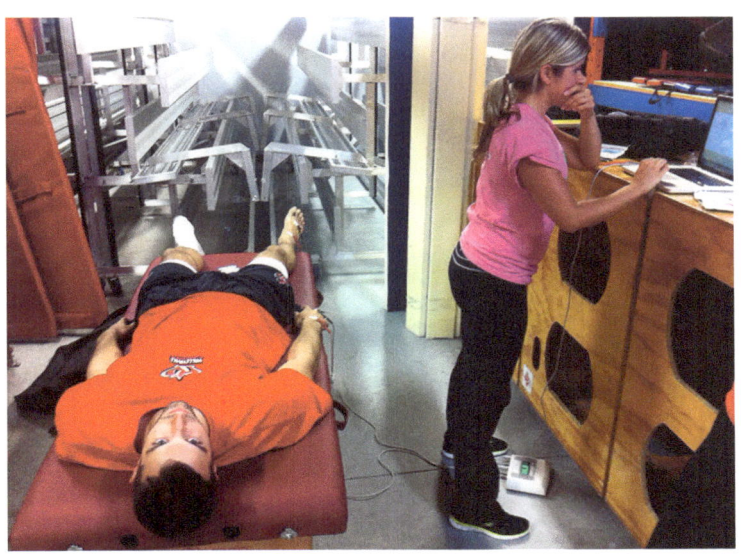

Basal Metabolic Rate: Basal metabolic rate (BMR) is the number of calories that are metabolized at rest during a 24-hour period.

Daily Energy Expenditure: DEE is an estimate of the calories a player burns through activities such as training. Naturally, DEE varies with the frequency and intensity of these activities.

Fat: This is the total amount of fat, calculated both in pounds and as a percentage of bodyweight.

Fat Free Mass: FFM is the weight of organs and muscles, including the water they contain and the weight of the bones. This data is available in pounds or as a percentage of bodyweight. An increase of FFM indicates either an increase in bone density or an increase in water. An increase in water can result from better hydration, or it may be caused by sarcoplasmic hypertrophy, glycogen storage, or inflammation. (More data is needed to understand what's actually going on.)

Lean Dry Mass: LDM is the quantity of muscle mass (without water) measured in pounds, as a percentage of bodyweight, and as a percentage of FFM. You want this number to increase to gain muscle hypertrophy.

Total Body Water (TBW) is contained in FFM, and consists of two components: intracellular water (ICW) and extracellular water (ECW). The amount of liquid inside the body is measured in pounds, as a percentage of bodyweight, and as a percentage of FFM. The amount of TBW should be at 69 percent or above of FFM. If it isn't, the player is dehydrated and conductivity is poor, which can cause an overestimate or underestimate of other parameters. Therefore, TBW is the first parameter that must be checked to determine whether other results are reliable.

Intracellular Liquid: ICL is the liquid inside cells. A perfect balance of minerals among magnesium, sodium, and potassium would give a 60 percent ratio of TBW.

Extracellular Liquid: ECL is the liquid outside cells. A perfect balance of minerals among magnesium, sodium, and potassium would give a 40 percent ratio of TBW. If ICL and ECL are not well balanced in these percentages, the player will experience a lack of energy very quickly during or after training, and recovery will be much tougher.

A high PA is consistent with large quantities of intact cell membranes and body cell mass.

Volleyball players with a better PA have a better capacity to train on the court or in the weight room. To have a good PA, the player needs to eat well to reduce inflammation, and consuming good fat is paramount for this. So telling volleyball players to reduce fat without distinguishing between the *types of fat* is a disservice. Most volleyball players we tested started with a PA of 6 or 7. For optimal results, adult men should be between 10 and 12 and adult women between 8 and 10. Below is a copy of my own results.

Nicolas Roy, Age 32, Male, Ht: 183 cm Wt: 183 lbs.						08/14/2014
RESISTANCE	REACTANCE	FRAME	TARGET	ACTIVITY	EQUATION	
413.5 Ω	67.7 Ω	MEDIUM	190 lbs.	LIGHT	ATHLETIC	
CURRENT TEST DATA						
WEIGHT			183.0 lbs.			
FAT			26.4 lbs.	14.4%		
FAT-FREE MASS (FFM)			156.6 lbs.	85.6%	% of FFM	
LEAN DRY MASS			38.7 lbs.	21.1%	24.7 %	
TOTAL BODY WATER (TBW)			117.9 lbs.	64.4%	75.3 %	% of TBW
INTRA-CELLULAR WATER			69.4 lbs.	37.9%	44.3 %	58.9 %
EXTRA-CELLULAR WATER			48.5 lbs.	26.5%	31.0 %	41.1 %
BMI 24.8	Basal Metabolic Rate 2011.9kCal					
Phase Angle 9.3	Daily Energy Expenditure 3219.1kCal					

The bonus section of this chapter online at defyinggravityvolleyball.com features a graph with the statistics of several players who were preparing to turn pro in Volleyball Canada's full-time center. The data is anonymous, but it gives you an idea of the results we typically see.

WHAT'S WRONG WITH THE STANDARD AMERICAN DIET?

When it comes to work capacity and nutrition, one problem is the standard American diet, which involves consuming foods from the four main food groups: vegetables and fruits, grains, dairy and substitutes, and meat and substitutes. Here's an example from Canada's food guide.[26] At the time of this writing (late 2014), its recommendations include:

Men:

- Vegetables and fruits: 8 portions for 14- to 18-year-olds and 8-10 portions for 19- to 50-year-olds.
- Grains: 7 portions for 14- to 18-year-olds and 8 portions for 19- to 50-year-olds.
- Dairy and substitutes: 3-4 portions for 14- to 18-year-olds and 2 portions for 19- to 50-year-olds.
- Meat and substitutes: 3 portions for 14- to 18-year-olds and 3 portions for 19- to 50-year-olds.

Women:

- Vegetables and fruits: 7 portions for 14- to 18-year-olds and 7-8 portions for 19- to 50-year-olds.
- Grains: 6 portions for 14- to 18-year-olds and 7 portions for 19- to 50-year-olds.
- Dairy and substitutes: 3-4 portions for 14- to 18-year-olds and 2 portions for 19- to 50-year-olds.

---

[26] www.hc-sc.gc.ca/fn-an/food-guide-aliment/basics-base/quantit-eng.php

- Meat and substitutes: 2 portions for 14- to 18-year-olds and 2 portions for 19- to 50-year-olds.

The biggest problem with the standard American diet is that two of the four food groups are questionable health choices. As documented in the best-selling book *Nutrition and Physical Degeneration* by Dr. Weston A. Price,[27] profound changes in the environment (e.g., in diet and lifestyle conditions, which began with the introduction of agriculture and animal husbandry about 10,000 years ago), occurred too recently on the evolutionary time scale for the human genome to adjust. Thanks to this "disconnect" between our ancient, genetically determined biology and the transformation of our food supply, many of the so-called diseases of civilization have emerged. In particular, food staples and food-processing procedures introduced in the Neolithic and Industrial Periods fundamentally altered seven crucial components of our ancestral diet: 1) glycemic load, 2) fatty acid composition, 3) macronutrient composition, 4) micronutrient density, 5) acid-base balance, 6) sodium-potassium ratio, and 7) fiber content. The evolutionary collision of our ancient genome with the nutritional qualities of recently introduced foods may underlie many chronic diseases of Western civilization,[28] including:

- -Musculoskeletal pain conditions
- -Rheumatoid Arthritis
- -Osteoporosis
- -Metabolic Syndrome

---

[27] amazon.com/Nutrition-Physical-Degeneration-Weston-Price/dp/0916764206

[28] ajcn.nutrition.org/content/81/2/341.full

THE STANDARD AMERICAN DIET

- -Type 2 Diabetes
- -Hypertension
- -Dyslipidemia
- -Coronary Heart Disease
- -Alzheimer's Disease

WHAT PROMOTES INFLAMMATION?

- -Standard American diet
- -Lack of omega-3 fatty acids and excess of omega-6 and saturated fat
- -Refined carbs/sugars and insulin resistance
- -Lack of plant-based phytonutrients
- -Excess weight and obesity
- -Food sensitivities: IgE, IgG, IgA, other
- -Chronic infections
- -Unhappy gastrointestinal flora
- -Chronic stress

What's wrong with grains?

Most grains have a higher glycemic load than fruits and vegetables. The glycemic load (GL) of food is an estimate of how much the food will raise a person's blood glucose level. One unit of glycemic load approximates the effect of consuming one gram of glucose. Glycemic load accounts for how much carbohydrate is in the food and how much each gram of carbohydrate in the food raises blood glucose level.[29] Many people use glycemic index tables to choose the carbohydrate value of what they eat, but tables are not very accurate. The glycemic index ranks how quickly sugar enters the bloodstream after a

---

[29] www.glycemic.com/GlycemicIndex-LoadDefined.htm

particular carbohydrate is eaten. It doesn't take into consideration the weight or the amount of carbohydrates in the food.

Glycemic load is much more accurate because it's a glycemic index-weighted measure of carbohydrate content.[30] It takes into account not only how quickly a certain food is converted into sugar, but also how much sugar a particular food contains. Using the glycemic load measure gives us a better estimate of how much insulin is secreted after eating a food. If too much is secreted because of the high glycemic load produced by (say) pasta, corn tortillas, and other grain-based foods, blood sugar will be directed to the muscles or liver very quickly – an aggressive fluctuation in blood sugar (hyperglycemia to hypoglycemia) that causes sugar cravings and sudden drops of energy.

Some studies have identified insulin as *the aging hormone.*[31] Given the epidemic of type 2 diabetes, as well as research showing that Alzheimer's disease is actually type 3 diabetes, it may be wise to choose foods with a moderate to low glycemic load to limit insulin secretion.

Some dieticians argue that grains help create the glycogen needed for high performance in sports. This is why some athletes are raving fans of pasta or rice before training.

The notion that you need a lot of carbs for performance is very strong in all sports, but endurance sports have contributed most to this mentality. The problem is that endurance sports use mostly aerobic systems, but sports like volleyball mostly use anaerobic

---

[30] cavemancircus.com/2014/01/03/hell-putting-bodies-truth-food-eating/
[31] www.ncbi.nlm.nih.gov/pmc/articles/PMC2769828/

systems. An anaerobic sport involves short, intense bursts of energy, which doesn't require as much glycogen as an aerobic sport because energy use isn't as *sustained*. When doing an anaerobic sport, you don't need the same amount of glycogens as you do for an aerobic sport. Therefore, carb-centric mentality does a disservice to many anaerobic athletes.

While it's true that we need carbohydrates to create glycogen (and we need glycogen to generate enough energy for sports), fruits and vegetables – especially the starchy ones like carrots, potatoes, beets – also produce glycogen. For more information, read *The Paleo Diet for Athletes* by Loren Cordain and Joe Friel.[32]

When I work with athletes in the morning, I can tell when they've eaten too many carbs, usually toast or breakfast cereals, because they'll be starving by the end of the session. Eating cereals and bread is similar to eating a candy bar: you'll feel full and energized for a short time, and then your glycemic level will crash.

Grains, legumes and dairy products also contain lectins – sticky molecules that can bind to the linings of human tissue, especially intestinal cells. In so doing, they disable cells in the GI tract, which prevents them from repairing and rebuilding. Lectins can erode your intestinal barrier, which can lead to "leaky gut."[33] It's common for a volleyball player to have a leaky gut caused by allostasis (adaptation to stress), because training can cause a lot of stress.

Leaky gut affects cell health – something we often detect in the PA results of the RJL BIA test – and it may

---

[32] thePaleodiet.com/dr-loren-cordain/
[33] institutefornaturalhealing.com/2009/07/lectins-a-little-known-trouble-maker/

lead to certain autoimmune diseases.[34] Because lectins circulate throughout the bloodstream, they can bind to any tissue in the body – e.g., the thyroid, pancreas, and the collagen in joints. This can trigger an autoimmune response in which white blood cells attack (and destroy) lectin-bound tissue. The lectins in wheat, for example, are known to be involved in rheumatoid arthritis. Meanwhile, autoimmune thyroiditis may be caused by dietary lectins.[35]

Basically, when food travels to the intestines, it *should* stay there to be digested. With leaky gut, however, some of the food enters the bloodstream without being digested. When this happens, your immune system attacks the food, thinking it's an unwanted intruder.

Leaky gut has many symptoms, including feeling bloated after meals and experiencing a lack of energy.

Why do some people react to the lectins in foods while others suffer no (obvious) adverse effects? The key word is "obvious." Many people may be suffering damage without realizing it because they have no symptoms. Many of our athletes who thought they had no food intolerance have experienced much-improved energy and weight control after eliminating wheat and dairy from their diets. They didn't notice the negative impacts of these foods until they quit eating them.

Finally, grains don't contain many vitamins and minerals. That's why commercial food manufacturers "enrich" grains with vitamins and minerals. Unfortunately, they enrich in ways that are less than

---

[34] todaysdietitian.com/newarchives/021313p38.shtml
[35] wellnessalternatives-stl.com/the-effect-of-dietary-lectins-on-thyroid-tsh-receptors/

THE STANDARD AMERICAN DIET

optimal. For example, they enrich cereals with *iron in its metal form,* which is not assimilated by the body.[36]

The other problem with grains is that they don't offer B6 and B12 vitamins unless they are enriched with these vitamins. And even if they *are* enriched, the anti-nutrients (such as lectins and phytic acid) in the grains will lower or even inhibit the vitamin absorption. A lack of B6 and B12 vitamins increases homocysteine (a form of inflammation), which increases the risk of heart attack.

Grains are acidic

Almost all foods are acidic – except fruits, vegetables, and clean water. I'm not referring here to the pH value of *undigested* foods, but to the level of acidity they generate in the body after digestion. For example, while fruits such as tomatoes, limes, and lemons are acid, that acidity is neutralized during digestion. On the other hand, while milk and dairy projects are only slightly acidic (or even neutral), they tilt the body's pH level into the "acid zone."

Your system should be alkaline or neutral. That's why eating vegetables and fruits and drinking water is so good for your health. If your body is acidic, it will compensate to bring itself to neutral. However, that process may come at a price: demineralization. Although his findings aren't universally accepted, Nobel Laureate Otto Heinrich Warburg[37] has shown that cancer can't develop in an alkaline environment. It needs an acidic environment. I don't know whether this is scientifically correct, but one

---

[36] naturalnews.com/043633_wheaties_cereal_metal_fragments_magnetic.html

[37] sites.google.com/site/ganodermareview/the-root-cause-of-cancer

thing is certain: research suggests that certain illnesses *are* more likely to arise in acidic environments.

Fibers

Some dieticians argue that whole grains are beneficial because they provide a good source of fiber – something many people lack. That's true. However, vegetables and fruits *also* provide soluble fibers in good quantities, without producing the negative effects that can come from eating grains.

Although it's not popular with the food industry, recent studies suggest that dietary fiber might not be as important as the food industry's marketing campaigns would have us believe.[38] In the report "Stopping or reducing dietary fiber intake reduces constipation," published in the *World Journal of Gastroenterology*, researchers put forth evidence that ancestral Inuits didn't eat much fiber and didn't experience the constipation problems or colorectal cancer that's so prevalent today[39] We "want to believe in the power of fiber," said Dr. Georgia Ede. "It is so much easier and so much more appealing to contemplate adding fiber, which is tasteless and indigestible, than to contemplate subtracting refined carbohydrates, which are both addictively delicious and fun to eat."[40]

Gluten

Despite all the hype about gluten-free products, gluten is still very popular. However, if you choose to eat

---

[38] ajcn.nutrition.org/content/91/2/295.full
[39] www.ncbi.nlm.nih.gov/pmc/articles/PMC3435786/
[40] www.diagnosisdiet.com/food/fiber/

THE STANDARD AMERICAN DIET

gluten-free, you're making a good decision. Even among people who don't have celiac disease (an autoimmune disorder of the small intestine), gluten promotes inflammation, which in excess is never a good thing.

Why are dairy products bad for almost everybody?

Lactose: Like other mammals, most humans gradually lose the intestinal enzyme lactase after infancy – and with it, the ability to digest lactose, the principal sugar in milk. Whenever the lactose ingested exceeds the capacity of the intestinal lactase to split it into the simple sugars glucose and galactose (which are absorbed directly), it passes undigested to the large intestine.[41] And because the intestine doesn't produce lactase, this causes gas, cramps, diarrhea, or a bloated feeling.

Dairy products contain casein

Casein: Even when people take lactase supplements to digest lactose, they may still encounter problems with casein, a protein contained in milk. Here's why. Milk consists of three parts: butterfat, whey, and milk solids. We're concerned with just one of the many proteins found in milk solids – specifically, beta-casein.

All proteins are long chains of amino acids with "branches" coming off the main "trunk." Beta-casein is a chain of 229 amino acids with proline at position 67. At least, that's where the proline is in ancient breeds of cattle such as Jerseys, Guernseys, and Asian and African cows, which are known as A2 cows. Some five thousand

---

[41] ajcn.nutrition.org/content/48/4/1079.2.short

years ago, however, a mutated form of beta-casein appeared in some of the animals. These are known as A1 cows, and they include modern breeds such as Holsteins and Friesians.

Put simply: the milk of newer A1 cows contains BCM 7, a small protein that acts as a powerful opiate (heroin and morphine are opiates). Unsurprisingly, this can produce undesirable effects on both animals and humans.

Keith Woodford describes research showing that BCM 7 can cause neurological impairment in the animals and people exposed to it, including autistic and schizophrenic changes. BCM 7 interferes with the immune response, and injecting BCM 7 into animals has been shown to induce Type 1 diabetes. Dr. Woodford also presents research showing a direct correlation between exposure to A1 cows' milk and the incidence of auto-immune disease, heart disease, type 1 diabetes, autism, and schizophrenia. In addition, BCM 7 selectively binds to the epithelial cells in the mucous membranes (like those in the nose), stimulating mucus secretion.[42]

Almost all American dairy cows have this mutated beta-casein because they are predominantly A1 cows.

Acidic: Like grains and meat, milk produces acidity in the body. Although calcium is important for bone growth and health, it's also important to understand two things. First, in addition to consuming *enough* calcium, our bodies need to eliminate *excess* calcium, because too much calcium (like too much of anything) isn't healthy. Second, two things eliminate excess calcium: sodium and an acidic environment. (Because dairy products are acidic, they flush excess calcium from the body – up to a point.)

---

[42] westonaprice.org/book-reviews/devil-in-the-milk-by-keith-woodford/

THE STANDARD AMERICAN DIET

Calcium: Many people worry that they won't have enough calcium for bone health if they don't consume dairy products. This is a myth. A meta-analysis of research on this topic found little or no relationship between dairy intake and measures of bone health.[43]

According to the Harvard School of Public Health, getting enough calcium from childhood through adulthood helps build bones *and* slow bone loss as we age. It's not clear, however, that we need as much calcium as many "experts" recommend. It's also not clear that dairy products are the best source of calcium for most people. Although the calcium in dairy products can lower the risk of osteoporosis and colon cancer, high amounts can increase the risk of prostate cancer and (possibly) ovarian cancer. In addition, dairy products can be high in saturated fat and retinol (vitamin A), which at high levels can actually *weaken* bones.

Good non-dairy sources of calcium include salmon, collards, bok choy, fortified soy milk, peas and beans, nuts and trail mix, and supplements that contain both calcium and vitamin D (a better choice than taking calcium alone). Limit milk and dairy foods to one to two servings per day. Having more won't necessarily do your bones any good – and less is fine, as long as you get enough calcium from other sources. Calcium-rich non-dairy foods also include leafy green vegetables and broccoli, both of which are also great sources of vitamin K, another key nutrient for bone health.[44]

---

[43] pediatricsdigest.mobi/content/115/3/736.short
[44] www.hsph.harvard.edu/nutritionsource/what-should-you-eat/calcium-and-milk/

However, if you choose to get your calcium from green leafy vegetables, beware of eating only spinach or rhubarb. The Linus Pauling Institute at Oregon State University notes that calcium-rich plants in the kale family (broccoli, bok choy, cabbage, mustard, and turnip greens) contain components that have been found to inhibit calcium absorption. Oxalic acid (also known as oxalate) is the most potent inhibitor of calcium absorption, and it's found at high concentrations in spinach and rhubarb and somewhat lower concentrations in sweet potatoes and dried beans.[45]

For more information about milk, read:

- *MILK – The Deadly Poison* by Robert Cohen and Jane Heimlich[46]
- Devil in the Milk: Illness, Health and the Politics of A1 and A2 Milk by Keith Woodford and Thomas Cowan[47]

Post-workout drink?

When dieticians recommend chocolate milk as a post-workout-recovery drink because of its perfect carbohydrate-to-protein ratio of 3-to-1, think twice! This ratio might be great for recovery, but chocolate milk is pro-inflammatory. To improve recovery, your entire biochemical profile must be considered, and that includes reducing inflammation.

---

[45] lpi.oregonstate.edu/infocenter/minerals/calcium/
[46] amazon.com/Milk-Deadly-Poison-Robert-Cohen/dp/0965919609
[47] amazon.com/Devil-Milk-Illness-Health-Politics/dp/1603581022

Thoughts on the Paleo Diet

Eating a Paleo diet means obtaining calories from lean meat, nuts, vegetables and fruits – and any other food a caveman could eat. The books *Primal Body, Primal Mind* and *Primal Blueprint* are good sources of information about the advantages of eating Paleo. The Paleo diet includes more fruits and vegetables than the average American diet, and also increases or stabilizes lean protein. This diet will improve biochemistry, especially if you eat organic foods, which contain fewer or no pesticides, fungicides, and GMOs. Keep in mind, however, that eating organic is often more expensive than eating the fruits and vegetables raised by industrial agriculture.

One reason for adopting a Paleo diet (in whole or in part) is to avoid or minimize processed and transformed foods. In terms of nutrient density – especially micronutrients, vitamins and minerals – there's a big difference between the minimally processed wild plants our ancestors ate and the highly processed, refined foods we consume today. Although many people are concerned about getting enough macronutrients such as fat, carbs, and protein, they tend to forget about the *micro*nutrients – the vitamins and minerals, especially minerals. Plenty of people focus on vitamins, but minerals? We hear almost *nothing* about them, despite their importance to health. People in our society are mostly deficient in minerals, and that's what creates so many biochemical problems. Our genes can adapt to the environment, but are our bodies keeping pace with the rate at which we're transforming our food? I don't think so.

I'm not talking about adapting to whole grains over the course of 10,000 years. I'm talking about adapting to highly refined, processed, grain-based foods over the last 50 to 100 years. Today's crops are not raised in the same ways they were just 50 to 100 years ago. For example, there is much more gluten in wheat *now* than there was 10,000 years ago. Today's industrial-style agriculture produces foods that are nothing like those eaten by your great-grandparents in terms of nutritional composition.

I don't eat perfectly Paleo. I sometimes eat gluten-free grains such as quinoa for glycogen purposes. However, because I'm aware of the problems associated with non-Paleo foods, I severely limit my intake. My diet consists of good fats, high-quality meat, vegetables, fruits, nuts, and sometimes gluten-free grains. When I eat grains and nuts, I soak them in water for a few hours to reduce the amount of phytic acid they contain. Most volleyball players are deficient in micronutrients such as magnesium and zinc – and phytic acid reduces the absorption of micronutrients.

In my opinion, the Paleo diet is a very good diet. However, it poses a few problems. First, if you really need lots of glycogen, you're out of luck. Marathon runners and other endurance athletes would have a problem with this diet. Second – and more importantly – there isn't enough Paleo food on the planet to adequately feed everyone. If everyone on Earth wanted to eat Paleo, a great many people would starve, because so much agriculture is now focused on producing corn, wheat, and soy – not vegetables, fruits, and nuts.

Third, thanks to soil poverty, many of today's Paleo foods do not contain enough micronutrients to meet the RDA unless you were to eat ridiculously large amounts of them. In the book, *Naked Calories*, Dr. Jayson Calton

THE STANDARD AMERICAN DIET

shows that the U.S. Paleo dieter would need to consume 14,000 calories daily to meet the RDA of all vitamins and minerals. The American average dieter would need to eat 27,000 calories for the same result!

What kind of diet is prescribed to our athletes?

We recommend mostly meat, fruits, and vegetables. However, our players don't eat perfectly Paleo. They're allowed to eat grains, such as quinoa for glycogen purposes, especially before big trainings. They're also allowed to use oil with their food because it's great for cell membranes.

The strict Paleo Diet philosophy doesn't accept quinoa, even though it's an alkaline grain full of great amino acids. It also doesn't accept vegetable oils because the Omega-6 to Omega-3 ratio is too high and because cavemen didn't have access to these. Although this is true, we ask our players to take a lot of Omega-3, so the ratio is improved and inflammation is kept low.

Our diet is not quite Paleo but neither is it a Mediterranean Diet. Even though we recommend oils and fruits and vegetables, we don't allow the athletes to eat cheese, and we insist that they be *very* moderate with their intake of grains. Whatever you want to call it, the diet works very well with our players.

Nutritional supplements: gimmick or necessity?

Many dieticians claim that if you eat properly, supplements aren't necessary.

Once upon a time, I supported this position – until I realized that supplements can improve both health and performance.

A few years ago, I was in a slump. I was tired, I was stressed, and I wasn't performing as well as I once had. My first thought was "Am I just aging?" So I did a few tests, and discovered that my testosterone level was decreasing. Why? Because my cortisol, which is the stress hormone (and antagonistic to testosterone) was too high.

Next, a professional tested my zinc level, which is a mineral and micronutrient, and he discovered that it was very low. Testosterone, like many other hormones, is created with zinc. In response, I reduced my stress using different techniques, including meditation. I also took a natural supplement to decrease cortisol secretion, and I took a zinc supplement to increase testosterone level. As a result, my performance improved significantly without much change in my nutrition. In fact, after taking these measures, I began beating my own personal records.

There are four main reasons that a well-fed volleyball player might need supplements:

1. We don't lead a Paleolithic-Era lifestyle. Few people today get *nearly* as much exercise as their ancient ancestors, and even fewer spend most of their time outdoors with regular access to sunlight, which is required for the production of vitamin D. Dairy products are enriched with vitamin D, but as I noted before, there are good reasons to reduce or eliminate these foods.
2. Large-scale industrial farming has reduced the amount of vital micronutrients (vitamins and minerals) in the soil.[48] The connection between

---

[48] www.sciencedirect.com/science/article/pii/S0946672X05000362

THE STANDARD AMERICAN DIET

    micronutrient-poor soil and inadequate nutrition is well documented.

3. The pesticides and fungicides we absorb from factory-farm products push our metabolisms to expend more micronutrients and phytonutrients on detoxifying our bodies.[49] Diet is a key factor in determining genomic stability – a factor more important than previously imagined – including the activation/detoxification of carcinogens, DNA repair, DNA synthesis and apoptosis (also known as "programmed cell death"). The current recommended dietary allowances for vitamins and minerals are based largely on the prevention of diseases of deficiency, such as scurvy. However, because diseases of development, degeneration, and aging are partly caused by damage to DNA, we should focus more on determining which key minerals and vitamins we need to best prevent damage to our DNA.

4. Allostasis is the body's adaptation to stress. (Homeostasis means remaining stable by staying the same, while allostasis means remaining stable by changing. Allostasis requires more micronutrients. People experience psychological stress from burdensome responsibilities and information overload. These stressors are the imaginary "lions" that trigger our primitive "fight or flight" urge – as opposed to the actual lions that stressed our ancestors. People also endure physical stress because of pollution, as our bodies must continually fight to detoxify. And for volleyball players and other athletes, stressors from the physical training load add to allostasis.

---

[49] www.ncbi.nlm.nih.gov/pmc/articles/PMC3114826/

Type 1 allostatic overload occurs when energy demand exceeds the supply, which causes your body to enter "survival mode," decreasing the allostatic load to help you regain a positive energy balance.

Type 2 allostatic overload occurs when there is sufficient or even excess energy accompanied by social conflict or other dysfunction. If your allostatic load is chronically high, various illnesses may develop. Type 2 allostatic overload does not trigger a "flight" response, and can be counteracted only by adapting to your social environment or by changing that environment.[50]

Below is a good image of allostatic load and its health implications vis-à-vis your ability to train. It was prepared courtesy of Jeffrey Moss, DDS, DACBN (www.mossnutrition.com).

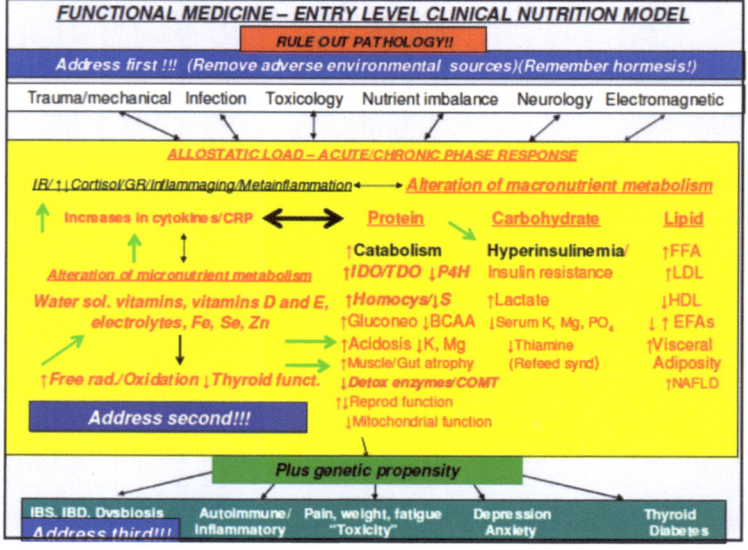

---

[50] www.ncbi.nlm.nih.gov/pubmed/12614627

THE STANDARD AMERICAN DIET

The goal is not to completely understand the allostatic incidence graph, but to be aware of it. Because volleyball players and other athletes can't change the social structure of competition – it's the name of the game – or the other three factors that negatively impact the body, supplements can be a great tool for helping players cope with allostatic load, improve work capacity and better tolerate a bigger training load (volume, intensity, density, and frequency).

If we agree that natural supplements might be beneficial to volleyball players, the next question is "Which supplements should volleyball players take?" The answer is: it depends, but let's look at a few essentials.

Omega-3: Most of us eat mammals and birds fed only with grains. Because of their diet, their meat contains many more Omega-6 fatty acids, which are pro-inflammatory, and far fewer Omega-3 fatty acids, which are anti-inflammatory. Unless you eat only wild fish and game, your Omega-3 to Omega-6 ratio will probably be too low to maintain adequate cell health. Unfortunately, eating grass-fed (or wild) meat and fish can be very costly, and the food industry can't supply these foods to everyone.

Vitamin D3: Known as the "sun vitamin" because it is synthesized through the skin, Vitamin D is found in dairy products such as milk in its D2 form, which is very difficult for the body to absorb. Dairy products contain added vitamin D because of many of us don't get enough exposure to UV rays to create enough vitamin D through other means. This poses a dilemma. If you stop consuming dairy products to improve your biochemistry, where do you get enough vitamin D? In winter, you'll need to take a supplement of the vitamin in its D3 form. You might also need it if you train indoors during the summer.

B Vitamins and greens: If you don't eat enough vegetables, you might need this supplement to keep your system more alkaline and to maintain enough B-vitamins, which are anti-inflammatory and contain antioxidants that fight the free radicals caused by pollution.

Magnesium: This is the micronutrient missing in almost everyone's diet, but especially in athletes because they lose so much through perspiration. The widespread poverty of agricultural soil is also responsible for the lack of magnesium in our diets. Magnesium contributes to cellular membrane permeability for energy creation and for muscle relaxation. According to Dr. Mark Sircus, magnesium deficiency is often misdiagnosed because it doesn't show up in blood tests. (Only one percent magnesium is stored in the blood, and most doctors and laboratories don't even test for it in routine blood tests, so doctors often don't know that their patients are deficient in magnesium.) According to Dr. Norman Shealy, "Every known illness is associated with a magnesium deficiency."

Zinc is important for hormone production, enzymatic reactions, and protein digestion for recovery. At Volleyball Canada, we test orally for zinc deficiency. (Note: taking too much zinc will eliminate copper.) Dr. Jeffrey Bland, in his article "Warning system within your hair," noted that human hair provides a continuous record of what's been going on in the body – a kind of nutritional microscope. Trace minerals are now getting the attention that vitamins did in the 1930s and '40s with regard to establishing proper health. We now recognize that of the 50+ nutrients essential for proper nutrition, many are in the family called the essential trace minerals. Some of these are cobalt, molybdenum, vanadium, selenium, chromium, and manganese. Each of these metals has roles in optimizing physiological function, mostly in facilitating processes associated with the body's enzymes. For instance, zinc is known to activate many enzymes, including DNA-dependent RNA polymerase – the enzyme that controls cell growth and repair. Copper is part of the enzyme ferroxidase, which is associated with the proper function of red blood cells. Shortages of these essential trace minerals can lead to reduced cell efficiency, which may result in disease or infection.[51]

Nutrigenomics perspective

Other natural supplements can help improve health and promote recovery and performance. However, you need to find a professional to assess your biochemical state – someone familiar with natural products. Many manufacturers sell supplements full of chemicals that can harm more than help. In addition, volleyball players, like many athletes, must be careful that the supplements they take won't produce false positives on drug tests.

For example, creatine, pre-workout formulas, and weight-gainer formulas can be risky for cross-contamination. In addition, we never give pre-workout formulas to our athletes because these products activate the adrenal glands, and in most athletes, the adrenal glands (which secrete cortisol) are already stressed for

---

[51] hookedonraw.com/shopping/articles/art_hairanalyses.html

the reasons mentioned above. The last thing we want is to stress them out even more.

As a rule, look for supplements with the National Sanitation Foundation (NSF) label on the package. That said, the NSF label doesn't *guarantee* the best quality. It only guarantees the product is drug-free. Some smaller brands without the NSF label actually use better ingredients in their formulas.

For more information, read *The Supplement Pyramid* by Dr. Michael A. Smith, senior health scientist and online personality for Life extension.[52]

I'm in favor of supplements, but from a nutrigenomics perspective. Nutrigenomics is a branch of nutritional genomics, which studies the effects of foods and food constituents on gene expression. Nutrigenomics research [53] seeks to identify and understand the molecular-level interactions between nutrients and other dietary chemicals with the genome. Put simply: the field hopes to develop ways to optimize nutrition vis-à-vis your individual genotype.

PERSPECTIVES

Many sports dieticians discourage athletes from taking supplements. Why? Because they have trouble distinguishing supplementation from doping. In my opinion, some people lump supplements in the same category as performance-enhancing drugs because it's easier for them to categorize all non-food products as

---

[52] amazon.com/Supplement-Pyramid-Personalized-Nutritional-Regimen/dp/1591203732

[53] en.wikipedia.org/wiki/Nutrigenomics

"bad." Unfortunately, some people don't take the time to educate themselves about the matter, so they dismiss all supplements as "drugs."

For me, a supplement is a natural product that enhances your nutritional intake and optimizes your body's function. The ingredients in the supplements are already found or supposed to be found in your food. You're simply adding more of them. By contrast, doping introduces external molecules (such as synthetic hormones or synthetic hormone precursors) that would not be produced by your body – at least, not in any significant quantities – without taking the drugs.

Again, it's a matter of education and perspective. Some dieticians claim that supplements are bad, but then encourage athletes to drink Gatorade for glycogen, despite the fact that it's loaded with high-fructose corn syrup! This cheap sugar derived from corn is bad for your biochemistry, but it's widely accepted by society because the food lobby has done such an effective marketing job. Should we consider it a supplement? I don't know, but sadly, some very good supplements are often viewed with suspicion while Gatorade has been given a "free pass" – or is even viewed as a "healthy choice."

People have different physical needs

Keep in mind that each individual is different. Because of this, some people might react better to grains and dairy products at their non-transformed level. This is extremely rare nowadays, thanks to legislation regarding pasteurization and because industrial agriculture focuses on high production and low prices. Individuality in nutrition depends a lot on metabolic typing, which is detailed in a book called *The Metabolic Typing Diet* by William L. Wolcott and Trish Fahey.[54]

SUMMARY

This chapter was written as a response to numerous statements I've heard from dieticians speaking to audiences of athletes. Some professionals are already knowledgeable about improving biochemistry, health, and work capacity for your sport. The ultimate goal is to minimize the *internal* load on your body so you can better withstand the *external* load (volume, intensity, density, and frequency of training). If you want to know more about the topic, the Weston A. Price Foundation is a good and impartial source of information.

If you want to develop a healthy diet plan and need advice on improving your biochemical profile for better work capacity, I encourage you to seek out professionals. In my opinion, the best people are those with a holistic approach.

---

[54] amazon.com/The-Metabolic-Typing-Diet-Customize/dp/0767905644

ORCHESTRATING THE SYMPHONY

DIRECTOR OF THE ORCHESTRA

The strength coach is a musician in an orchestra and the head coach is the director.

Art and science

The main periodisation model of a volleyball team should be done by the head coach. When the head coach is aware of the importance of periodisation, which is not always the case, it works for the players and for the integrated support team (the orchestra). With Volleyball Canada, I have the privilege of working with Glenn Hoag and Vincent Pichette, both of whom excel at planning, and it's a pleasure working with the group dynamics. Planning by the strength coach is derived from the global planning of the head coach, because sports science must be at the service of volleyball and not the opposite. There are different efficient methods used in periodisation. Like a recipe, it's a mix of art and science between what is proven by science or empirical experience and what can be done in the context in which the volleyball team evolves.

Three principal aspects for performance

Apart from the technico-tactical aspect of planning in volleyball, a team usually wants to address three principal aspects in performing well:

Biochemistry of the player: The first step is to assess and improve the biochemical profile of the player to make sure she can tolerate the workload and recuperate well. If there's a leak (inflammation) in your house (GI system) caused by a broken water system (food creating inflammation), what do you do first? Do you put your hand in the sink and try to unblock it (medicine) or do you shut off the water supply (poor food choices)?

Psychological health of the player: Like postural testing and agility development and biochemistry, this topic would need a book of its own. Research, though, has proven that negative thoughts resulting from experiences that created psychological trauma create inflammation – and thus add to the allostatic load.[55] There are effective ways of countering psychological trauma or challenges, but a professional in the field should be consulted.

Biomechanical and physiological

Players' biochemical and physiological adaptations should be developed simultaneously. Let's now focus on the planning aspects of biomechanical and physiological adaptations to improve the physical state of preparedness for the game. In planning the training process, I usually go from general to specific exercises for a planned timeframe.

Depending on the context, which includes the players I work with and the competition calendar, I do structural balance exercises in a moderate-to-high density (work duration to rest duration ratio) parameter for a period of 2 to 6 weeks. This phase will sometimes include hypertrophy and work capacity aspects. During this structural balance phase, I use the philosophy and exercises presented in chapter 3 and 4.

---

[55] www.nature.com/npp/journal/v22/n2/full/1395453a.html

Be careful with specificity in strength training

After the initial phase I switch to specificity work. In strength training, I'm not a big fan of too much specificity. I prefer using effectivity rather then specificity. In my vocabulary and perception, first introduced to me by track and field coach Jean Laroche, effectivity is an exercise you can overload that is different from the sport's action. This overload will create adaptations that transfer well in the sport's action. According to supertrainer Dr. Mell Siff, there are ten aspects in which effectivity can be close to a sport's actions: type of muscle contraction, movement pattern, region of movement, velocity of movement, force of contraction, muscle fiber recruitment, metabolism, biochemical adaptation, flexibility, and fatigue.[56]

But, from my perspective, specificity is to overload a motion that is the same as the one used in the sport. Why do I avoid too much specificity? In Mel Siff's book *Supertraining* he refers to specificity as the terminology simulation: While simulation of a sporting movement with small added resistance over the full range of movement or with larger resistance over a restricted part of the movement range may be appropriate at certain stages of training, simulation of any movement with significant resistance is inadvisable, since it can confuse the neuromuscular programmes which determine the specificity of the above factors. Even if one is careful to apply simulation training by using implements or loads that are similar to those encountered in the sport, there will usually be changes in the center of gravity, moments

---

[56] www.drmelsiff.com

of inertia, centre of rotation, centre of percussion and mechanical stiffness of the system, which alter the neuromuscular skills required in the sport.[57]

Let's consider an arm swing attack for example. Exercises like pull-over, push-press, or Bradford press are *effective* for that movement, while doing arm swings with an elastic or a small plate are *specific* (simulation). Another example would be hang power clean, hang power snatch, and jerks as effective exercises to improve vertical jump or spike jumps with a resisted weight vest as a specific exercise to improve vertical jump. I prefer using effective exercises, which transfer very well and remove the risk of confusing the central nervous system. The next question is what periodisation model do I use? It depends.

Different periodisation models for different context

I usually work with different periodisation models depending on the context that the team is in for preparation to competition. The three planning models I like to use most are:

- Ondulatory model
- Conjugate method
- Delayed cumulative effects model

Ondulatory model

This model alternates between accumulation and intensification mesocycles. In accumulation cycles we

---

[57] supertraining-siff.com/pub.html

either improve or maintain strength endurance, hypertrophy, or speed strength endurance. In intensification mesocycles, we improve or maintain maximal strength, explosive strength, or reactive strength. Here's an example:

Weeks 1-2 : 8 repetitions (Accumulation)
Weeks 3-4 : 4 repetitions (Intensification)
Weeks 5-6 : 6 repetitions (Accumulation)
Weeks 7-8 : 2-3 repetitions (Intensification)
Weeks 9-10 : 5 repetitions (Accumulation)
Weeks 11-12 : 1-2 repetitions (Intensification)

During those week blocks (mesocycles), the number of repetitions is stable in every training for almost all exercises except for some auxiliary exercises that don't require as much intensity. The ondulatory model offers more flexibility than the delayed cumulative effects model, but less than the conjugate method. It's a good median option. This is the model I use with the Full Time Center (FTC) in Gatineau. The FTC is the camp that is held between September and April by Volleyball Canada to train athletes who are done with university's volleyball (CIS level) and want to reach the professional and international level. The players train a lot technically, tactically, and physically. Unfortunately, they don't have a lot of competitions, because there's no professional volleyball in North America. With this model, we plan so that competitions occur during the intensification phase, because during FTC they might go to the North America, Central America, and Caribbean volleyball championship (NORCECA) and to Europe for a training camp of two weeks. Usually, the athletes who perform well during the FTC are selected for the B team by mid-April and some of them get a professional contract the next year. We use this model with FTC players because the accumulation mesocycles don't affect competitions – because there is no competition schedule.

Because the A team is in World league and the competition calendar is much denser, we don't use this model as often as we did back when Canada wasn't in World league. We still sometimes use it, depending on the competition schedule.

Conjugate model

This is the most flexible of the models. The conjugate model is not my favorite to develop a certain physical quality, but when the competition schedule is dense like that of Volleyball Canada in summer 2014 with the World League and then the World Championships, this is the most practical. This model is a mix of dynamic efforts (explosive strength and reactive strength), maximal efforts (maximal strength), and repetitive efforts (hypertrophy and strength endurance). Each strength training day is based on one of these three categories, which are alternated throughout the week. This periodisation model is derived from the powerlifting culture, but we use it differently so that the technico-tactical aspect of the game is not hindered. In volleyball this technique maintains a good physical condition (optimisation) for slight improvements, but it offers less precise adaptations because it's a mix of physical qualities. If a player really needs a specific physical adaptation (maximisation) to improve her game, this method is not the best way to plan the physical training for her context.

Delayed cumulative effects model

This planning model requires experience in weight training, because the training methods used in this model are advanced. This model is very rarely used in volleyball. In fact, with Volleyball Canada, we used it only once and I have been working with the men's team for 5 years. We used this model for strength training in preparation for World Championships in 2010. It worked very well, but choosing this method was a risky decision. When I presented this technique to my colleague strength coach Michael Fullum, he tried it with a female volleyball player who had a good weight training background, because she was preparing for a selection camp. The results were astounding and the risks were less important than with Volleyball Canada. Why? The answer that I'm about to give you is what happened with our experience and is not backed by science – but it's worth a lot!

Best vertical jump improvement results

Using this method will give the best explosive and vertical jump improvement results, to this I can attest. However, it will happen in a very small and precise period, so you must be certain that the date of the competition won't change. Some leagues or volleyball organizations occasionally change their dates of competition. In that situation, this method has no flexibility, and the players would probably not be at their top physical state on the changed date. This method is much more useful for sports such as track and field, in which the technico-tactical aspect is less important than in volleyball. In fact I used it with track and field athletes before trying it with the men's national team in 2010 World's.

Two challenges with this technique

Two other challenges occur with this technique. We had to deal with both problems during the 2010 World championship preparation. First, the players might be less explosive during the process as close as 3 to 4 weeks before the main competition. I remember the team went to Slovenia for a training camp, playing other teams to prepare for the main competition, and they were totally flat. The head coach, the assistant coach, and the players were freaking out. But they said, "Let's continue and have faith in the process." Do I have to tell you I was nervous? Fortunately, it was a great success, and the guys were in their best shape at the Championship. In fact players who remember this experience still talk about it today like it was the best physical experience they ever encountered in competition. The second challenge with this method is that after the great results, the guys were lethargic for a while. The World championship was at the end of summer. Because of this delayed lethargy, the return of the players to their professional careers in the beginning of autumn was more difficult than usual.

How does this method work?

We chose this method of planning in 2010 because we had 12 weeks to prepare for the world championship, and we had no important volleyball competition scheduled during that period. Volleyball Canada didn't have enough money at that time to be part of World League. We also couldn't use this model for the following years, because we had a lot of competitions such as NORCECA or World League. This model is based on emphasizing contraction types while considering their cumulative delayed effects on physical preparedness from the period of the training until the period of the important event. How does this method work physiologically? Research seems nonexistent on this subject. I tried aggressively to find documents in English or in French to explain the reasons behind the protocol, but I didn't succeed. I found only a document in French, a course from a University where the same numbers as those I use were repeated without any explanation of the science behind the protocol. If you want to find it, search for "Méthodes de musculation. Planification et intérêt dans la pratique sportive Philippe Connes (MCU) Université des Antilles et de la Guyane." You'll come up with numerous search results.

DEFYING GRAVITY

THE PERIODISATION PROTOCOL

How did I develop this protocol?

About ten years ago, when I was starting my career with my former partner Lisandro Araneda, we tried a protocol found in a German book and it worked to a very impressive level! We used the protocol that is presented in a tab at page 274 in Jürgen Weineck's book *Manuel d'entraînement* (which means "Training Manual" in French). This book was translated from German to French by Professor Michel Portmann. [58] This periodisation model requires 12 weeks of aggressive training. If you want to do a 4-week phase of structural balance for a posturally better-balanced athlete, you need a context of 16 consecutive weeks in which the team doesn't compete – or where the competition results aren't that important. This is a rare situation, but in 2010, we had such a situation for a period of 12 weeks.

Weeks 12 to 10 from the championship

Eccentric accentuated method: The delayed effects are 10 to 12 weeks from the period of training, so I use this technique 12 to 10 weeks before the championship. During this phase, we used weight releasers or aggressive tempos such as single repetition of 10 seconds of eccentric phase (lowering).

Eccentric accentuated method contrasted with explosive or reactive effort: The delayed effects are 12 to

---

[58] Weineck, Jürgen. Manuel d'entraînement: physiologie de la performance sportive et de son développement dans l'entrainement de l'enfant et de l'adolescent. 4e éd. révisée et augmentée. ed. Paris: Editions Vigot, 1997.

10 weeks from the period of training, so I use this technique 12 to 10 weeks before the championship.

We mostly used the eccentric accentuated method contrasted to keep the speed strength component active if players are slow. However, for players who lack strength but are already very fast, I would put the emphasis on the eccentric overload only. This mesocycle has a 3-week duration. The volume is often regressive (diminishing each week) because this method generates nervous system fatigue.

Weeks 9 and 8 from the championship

Maximal isometric method: If I refer to the tab in the German book noted above, the delayed effects of maximal isometric efforts occur 9 weeks from the period of training. So, if you used the German document, you would use this technique 9 weeks before the championship. Because I want the mesocyle to last at least 2 weeks, I schedule it for weeks 9 and 8. There is no physical quality noted until week 6 in the document referring to delayed cumulative training effects. The intent of not writing anything for week 7 in that protocol is maybe to have a break at week 7 because the training process is really intense – I am not sure, but that is my theory. In fact, this German document focuses on a lot of physical qualities at week 6. It's almost overwhelming at that period.

Weeks 7 and 6 from the championship

The delayed effects are predicted for 6 weeks from the period of training. I use these methods for both weeks 7 and 6 before the championship because there's nothing written for week 7 in the original. However, I used a progressive volume for this mesocycle so that the volume

THE PERIODISATION PROTOCOL

at week 7 is low, to help the nervous system to rest. Volume was then increased at week 6.

Concentric accentuated method – described in the chapter showing the maximal strength methods contrasted with explosive or reactive efforts. In this method, I use elastics or chains attached to the bar to overload the concentric phase of the movement (squat or deadlift) and then I prescribe the contrast with a plyometric exercise (reactive strength) or an explosive strength action such as weightlifting derivatives, underhand medicine ball throw, or dumbbell triple extension motions.

Intensive plyometrics is also scheduled during this phase. Using drop jumps or consecutive hurdle jumps may be a good idea if the athlete is ready for it.

Total isometrics are those in which the load is submaximal, and you need to maintain it for a longer period than with maximal isometrics. This is tough psychologically. We didn't use this method a lot, except for postural work because it creates a lot of fatigue for technico-tactical training in volleyball.

Weeks 5 and 4 from the championship

This is a 2-week cycle (weeks 5-4 before the championship) where the method used is the 40-60 percent. In this method, we use intensities that are the equivalent of 40 to 60 percent of 1 R.M and do repetitions as fast as possible. The number of repetitions is decided by the speed of the movement. When the speed decreases to a certain amount (for example 10%), the player stops his set. Using a myotest device for this technique is very advantageous because the accelerometer brings a quantitative aspect that helps to take the decision to stop the set. If the player or the coach don't have access to this technology, we can use another great technique that was introduced to me by American weightlifting coach John Broz. In this technique, you use a 40 to 60 % of 1 R.M resistance and you do as many reps as you can in a 5 second period. If the number of reps drops too much (10 %) you stop even if the number of sets prescribed is not done yet.

Week 3 and 2 from the championship

This cycle has a 1- to 2-week duration (weeks 3 and 2). In this cycle, we use concentric overload, which can be done by using bands. This overload will increase acceleration potential by increasing the resistance simultaneously with the increase in the range of motion (strength curve). This technique also diminishes the delayed-onset muscle soreness effects, because the emphasis is not on the overload of the eccentric phase, which is in fact facilitated by the bands tension. I recommend using bands to avoid moving the strength/time curve, which is very important at this time. The volume should be kept low to moderate.

The last week before the championship

During this week we use no delayed effect. We use only immediate effect by including a low-volume and high-intensity technique such as the contrasted concentric method (with bands) to add it up to all the other delayed effects for the championship. At this time, the players are flying!

This is it for this technique. Be careful that you use it only with players who have a solid background in strength training.

THE PERIODISATION PROTOCOL

Linear model of planning

The linear model of planning emphasizes one physical quality for a mesocycle (2 to 4 weeks) that is a prerequisite for another physical quality, then shifting to this other physical quality in the following mesocycle of 2 to 4 weeks. For example, a coach would plan a training for hypertrophy for a duration of 4 weeks, then he would shift to maximal strength development for 4 weeks, and finally shift to speed-strength for 4 weeks. Judging by what I've seen, this model is very popular among coaches in Canada. This model can be useful for a beginner volleyball player who doesn't have much experience in strength training yet wants to improve his physical qualities in a progressive manner. This technique, though, will lead to plateaus for players with a broader strength training experience, because the duration of phases and the lack of recurrence in physical quality development or stabilization will lead to a detraining effect that will erode the basis. For example, hypertrophy is a prerequisite for strength training that is a prerequisite for speed strength training. If the speed strength phase is too long (some coaches avoid too much delayed-onset muscle soreness in favor of more quality on the court), the players will lose muscle hypertrophy and strength and thus speed-strength even if they train for this physical quality. This is why I don't exclusively use this basic periodisation model.

A matter of context

There are many other great philosophies and protocols for strength training in volleyball. When choosing the proper periodisation model, it's crucial that it fits with the context of the volleyball team you train. You might have the very best periodisation model to improve the physical qualities that you want to improve, but if it doesn't fit with your team's context, it will lead your team to failure. Even if the periodisation model was given to you by the best coach in the world, it doesn't matter. Some coaches have a tendency to over-complicate the topic of periodisation.

Periodization requires a lot of thought about your context and how to plan the training process to optimise results by embracing this context. It's not always easy, and it doesn't always follow the perfect scenario in accordance with physiology or neurology, but it should be the closest to that perfect scenario. Some young strength coaches sometimes want to change the team's context so that it fits with the perfect sports science scenario. Sometimes it is possible to change the team's context, but the higher the degree of competition of the team, the less it's possible because of too many factors including:

- Competition calendar (sometimes less than optimal)
- Travel calendar
- Access to training facilities with schedules (especially when on the road)
- Technico-tactical practice calendar
- Schedules of other professionals (physiotherapists, medical doctors, etc.)

Resilience

I remember when a strength coach who was new to the profession came with me to see Team Canada in Gatineau. This guy was a living training bible, and it was really fun to discuss approaches with him because he was

THE PERIODISATION PROTOCOL

fluent with training theory. However, when he looked at what was done with our team, he freaked out! He was seeing situations in which we could optimise the strength training and the recovery process. It was funny because the guy had so many solutions he was suggesting we implement immediately! Needless to say, while I was agreeing and aware of what he was telling me, I had to explain to him why what he was telling me couldn't be applied just now because of the contextual situation. The coach and I painted him the whole contextual picture, and then he understood. He said, "I would have difficulty working in that context because it's not perfect, and I like to control the whole context."

Resilience and flexibility with contextual challenges are necessary if you want to be good in periodisation with high-level volleyball teams – or with any other sport. Sports science is at the service of the sport team, not the other way around.

ACKNOWLEDGMENTS

First of all, I want to thank my wife Marie-Soleil because she is my friend, partner, and soulmate. Her great support really helped me to write this book.

Thanks to all the Fonctions Optimum team members: Michael Fullum, Fanny Beaudin, Francis Lapointe, Marie-Christine Grenier, David Foucher, Bruno Boivin, and my lovely wife Marie-Soleil Samson. The motivation and the inspiration that you provide me are immeasurable! It's a pleasure and an honour to work with you.

I'm also grateful for the direct and indirect help for the redaction of this book from Pierre-Luc Perreault, Jeffrey Moss, Martin P. Albert, Christian Thibaudeau, and my wife Marie-Soleil Samson.

Regarding the direct influence of my professional career as a strength and conditioning coach, I want to thank Jean Laroche, Daniel Mercier, Martin Roy, Christian Thibaudeau, Lisandro Araneda, Dave Marois, Brian Grasso, John Davies, and Lucie Blouin. You all influenced me and helped me become the professional that I am.

I want to thank all the staff working at the men's indoor Volleyball Canada program: Glenn Hoag, Vincent Pichette, Francis Boyer, Julien Boucher, all the physiotherapists from the team of Physio Outaouais, and all the volleyball players that I've had the chance to work with. Without you, this book cover and this book wouldn't exist. I really like working with you!

I want to thank Denis Fontaine and all the members of Vert et Or women's volleyball program from Université de Sherbrooke. Denis, keep doing what you do so well!

I want to thank Daniel Moreau, Jessica Lambert, Anne-Julie D'auteuil, Mathieu Courchesne, and Francis Lapointe, who are the models for the exercises pictured in this book. You are all great and good-looking athletes and this is why I'm proud that you agreed to represent this book!

I'm thankful to Annie Roberge for the photos of me that she took for the book cover. You are a great photographer! I'm also very grateful to Tristan Grégoire who designed the book cover. I really like it!

Thanks to my editor Kelly Andersson. You helped me so much to improve my manuscript and to bring it to book form. Thanks for your precious advice.

For writing consultation, my thanks to Peter Gerardo, who greatly helped with chapter clarity and reliability.

I want to thank author Raymond Aaron who helped me to produce this book and who inspired me to start the project. Without you, this book would have waited for another decade or more. I want to thank author Bill O'Hanlon, who helped me find the title of this book when I met him by pure coincidence. I really like it: *Defying Gravity*.

Finally, I want to thank my parents who helped me become the man that I am.

www.ingramcontent.com/pod-product-compliance
Lightning Source LLC
Chambersburg PA
CBHW041611220426
43669CB00001B/5